JIGSAW

JIGSAW –

A Political Criminology of Youth Homelessness

PAT CARLEN

OPEN UNIVERSITY PRESS
Buckingham • Philadelphia

Open University Press
Celtic Court
22 Ballmoor
Buckingham
MK18 1XW

and
1900 Frost Road, Suite 101
Bristol, PA 19007, USA

First Published 1996

A catalogue record of this book is available from the British Library

ISBN   0 335 19680 2 (pb)   0 335 19681 0 (hb)

Library of Congress Cataloging-in-Publication Date
Carlan, Pat.
     Jigsaw : a political criminology of youth homelessness / Pat Carlen.
        p.   cm.
     Includes bibliographical references and index.
     ISBN 0–335–19681–0   ISBN 0–335–19680–2 (pbk)
     1. Juvenile delinquents — Great Britain.   2. Homeless youth — Great
Britain.   3. Juvenile delinquency — Political aspects — Great Britain.
I. Title.
HV9145.A5C365   1996
364.3'6'0941–dc20
                                                            95–26512
                                                                CIP

Typeset by Type Study, Scarborough
Printed in Great Britain by St Edmundsbury Press,
Bury St Edmunds, Suffolk

CONTENTS

ACKNOWLEDGEMENTS

The major empirical investigation which provided the illustrative materials for this book was funded by the Economic and Social Research Council (ESRC). I therefore acknowledge with thanks ESRC Award No.R.000.23.3540 which funded the project entitled Young People, Lawbreaking, Criminalization and Homelessness in Three Central England Cities, 1992–1995 (joint grantholders 1992–1994, Pat Carlen and Julia Wardhaugh; sole grantholder 1994–1995, Pat Carlen). Throughout the book this research is referred to as the Three Cities Project. I also acknowledge with thanks Julia Wardhaugh's contribution (as Research Fellow) to the first two years of the empirical investigation.

Findings from a small project entitled the Shropshire Single Homelessness Survey, 1992 (grantholder, Pat Carlen) have also contributed to some of the ideas put forward in the following pages. For funding that survey I thank: Shropshire Probation Service, District of the Wrekin Council, Shrewsbury and Atcham Borough Council, Council of the Borough of Oswestry, Bridgnorth District Council, North Shropshire District Council, Telford Christian Council, Stonham Housing Association, and Adullam Homes Housing Association.

Many people gave unstintingly of their time and expert knowledge to help with both projects. In connection with the Three Cities Project, my thanks to the staff of the following hostels, agencies or projects: in Manchester, the City Council and Housing Department; Outreach; Shades; Big Issue; The Survivors' Project; Albert Kennedy Trust; Lifeshare; Manchester and Salford Methodist Mission; The Beeches; Manchester Crisis Centre; Stopover; Peterloo Housing Association, Direct Access; Housing Projects Advisory Service; Greater Manchester CHAR; Salford After Care Project (National Children's Home); Oldham Single Homeless Project; Greater Manchester Probation – Minshull Street Day Centre; New Beswick House; Oswald Road Hostel; Save the Children, North West; and NACRO Housing; in Birmingham, St Basil's Centre and associated hostels – New Boot, Yardley House, Tennyson House, Trentham House, and the Link; Central Methodist Church; West Midlands Police; NACRO; Shelter Housing Aid Centre; AIDS Line, West Midlands; Step Two; Birmingham Standing Committee for the

Single Homeless; Youth Link; HARP; McNeille House, Solihull; SHAPE; Birmingham Youth Service; Lighthouse Mission; Salvation Army; Focus Housing Association; South Birmingham Young Homeless Project; Trinity Housing Advice; and in Stoke-on-Trent, Granville House; Potteries Housing Association; Potteries Young Homeless Project; Resettlement Project North Staffs; YMCA, Edinburgh House; Salvation Army; St Mark's Night Shelter; Shelter Campaign for the Homeless at Burslem, Tunstall, and Longton; Rainbow Centre; Elizabeth Trust; Children's Society; Teen Challenge Christian Centre; Hanley Youth Project; Shelton Neighbourhood Centre; Citizens Advice Centre, Hanley; Department of Social Security, Hanley and Newcastle-under-Lyme; Staffordshire Alcohol Advisory Service; Druglink – North Staffs; Alcohol Advice Centre, Hanley; North Staffs Racial Equality Council; MIND, North Staffs; SAIVE; North Staffs Victim Support Scheme; Rape Crisis; Stoke-on-Trent City Council; Staffordshire Housing Association; North Staffordshire Housing Consortium; Staffordshire Police.

Denise at Centre Point in London was always very helpful and generous with her time, as were the probation staff at Stafford Prison and Brinsford Young Offenders Institution.

A special word of thanks is owed to Paul Bridges who was Research Assistant on the project for the two years 1993 to 1995. Paul conducted two-thirds of the interviews with the young homeless people and also helped produce some of the statistics.

In connection with the Shropshire Single Homelessness Survey, my thanks to: Julia Wardhaugh who conducted most of the interviews and helped with the 'sleeping rough' count; Dee Cook, who provided many of the initial contacts; 'Peter' who, although extremely busy looking for accommodation, and sleeping rough himself, acted as official enumerator for the 'sleeping rough' count in Bridgnorth; Hilary Knight of Wrekin Housing Task Force and Jenny Ayres of South Shropshire Young Persons Housing Project, who generously made available their own unpublished findings on homelessness in Shropshire; and Hillary Bradshaw, Ian Loader, John Law and Peter Carlen who all assisted with the 'sleeping rough' count.

Throughout the writing of this book I have had wonderful support from the members of the Keele Criminology Department – Mike Collison, Lynn Hancock, Tim Hope, Richard Sparks, Sandra Walklate, Anne Worrall, Anne Musgrave – and especially Ian Loader, who read every word of the typescript and whose criticism was always incisive and always valued. Jo Phoenix was generous in sharing with me her own PhD research findings on the links between homelessness and prostitution. Mark Lettiere at the University of California, Davis helped tremendously by alerting me to the most recent American work on homelessness; and various conversations with Ann Aungles, Daniel, Jill and Peter Carlen, Stan Cohen, Chris Hale, Shelly Messinger, Laurie Taylor and Jackie Tombs were inspirational.

I dedicate this book to the 150 young homeless people in Manchester, Birmingham, Stoke-on-Trent and Shropshire who took so much trouble to answer questions carefully and at length.

INTRODUCTION

Over 150,000 young, single adults are homeless in Britain. It is a statistic which shocks some people and terrifies others. Those who are shocked are surprised and saddened that at the end of the twentieth century so many British citizens are still living in the most punishing poverty; those who are terrified are haunted by fears of a corrosive Otherness – of a social, political and moral contagion that threatens their homes and personal security.

Jigsaw examines the political conditions which have shaped the forms, refractions and effects of youth homelessness today, showing how it is a very twentieth-century production, strangely caught in the tensions between late-modern systems of welfare regulation, postmodern creativities of identity risk and reflexivity, and persisting and premodern fears about the wanderer, the traveller, the mendicant – and all those Others who have chosen to live where they cannot be *addressed*.

But why a *political criminology* of youth homelessness? Primarily because the majority of young people who are homeless have been victims and survivors of policies on housing, welfare, and criminal justice that have especially targeted the young for close surveillatory regulation and punishment. One aim of the book, therefore, is to demonstrate how a critique of the relationships between punishment and politics can also inform a greater understanding of the relationships between homelessness, lawbreaking, punishment and new lifestyles . . . *but without reducing each of them to being always and already something other than they are.* Another aim is to present the distinct specificity of prevailing disciplinarities and innovative lifestyles associated with youth homelessness, at the same time as indicating their implications for the politics of youth citizenship and social change (cf. Katz 1989; Yeich 1994).

Asymmetries of citizenship and anti-social controls

A concern with the right of the state to inflict punishment on wrongdoers has been of recurring concern to penal philosophers, and questions of the democratic state's right to punish are necessarily bound up with issues of citizenship (see Carlen 1983b).

Contemporary justifications of the state's power to punish stem from the contract theories of, for example, Locke and Hobbes. In contract theory the right to punish is predicated upon a conceit that the state is founded upon the citizens' consensual agreement to surrender to state agencies their individual capacities to redress wrongs done to them. In return, citizens have a right to expect the state to protect their lives and property. In democratic societies the state agencies are themselves expected to be subject to due legal process. In welfare states, moreover, an expectation has also been raised that citizens will receive 'minimal need satisfaction' (Doyal and Gough 1991: 92). Thus a moral reciprocity is set up: the state is to satisfy the minimum needs of citizens and protect their lives and property from attack; citizens are to fulfil obligations to obey the law and to carry out other civic responsibilities laid upon them by virtue of their citizenship. In such a culture, argue Doyal and Gough (1991: 96),

> It must follow that a precondition for blaming *anyone* . . . for acting immorally and expecting them to do better in the future is respecting their right to the minimum level of need-satisfaction to enable them to do so.

In the following pages it will be shown that during the 1980s the British state failed to meet the minimum needs of increasing numbers of young citizens at the same time as targeting them for receipt of tighter disciplinary controls and, in the 1990s, even harsher punishments. During the same period it was revealed that while young persons suffer criminal victimization on a large scale, the crimes committed against them are seldom redressed. Young people themselves do not believe that police protection is extended to them in the same way that it is to older adults (especially older adults who are also householders), and they also feel excluded from debates about the forms, functions and possibilities of democratic policing. Instead of a moral reciprocity of citizen rights, there is an asymmetry of citizenship, with young people being punished for not fulfilling their citizenship obligations even though the state fails to fulfil its duties of nurturance and protection towards them.

At times when the juridical relations of citizenship are extremely asymmetrical, citizens forced to pay their penal dues without receiving any citizen dividends are likely to experience many state controls as anti-social and therefore illegitimate. For, whereas legitimate *social* control is comprised of a variety of benign institutionalized practices designed to set limits to individual action in the interests of the collectivity's ideals (as instanced in law and dominant ideologies), *anti-social* controls set limits to individual action by exploiting asymmetries of citizenship and thereby atrophying the subjugated citizenry's social contribution even more (see Carlen 1995a for a discussion of anti-social control).

Under the Thatcher governments of the 1980s the state's legitimacy was undermined by the mobilization of anti-social controls against certain sections of the population (e.g. the children of the poor, trade unionists and public sector workers) at the same time as the regulatory mechanisms controlling the economic behaviour of others (e.g. money marketeers, employers and private speculators) were removed. Social and economic inequality rapidly increased, and extremes of poverty and wealth were created. Fears among the conservative and social democratic middle classes about the emergence of a crimogenic 'underclass' (Dahrendorf 1985) were balanced by mounting concern in other quarters about the greed of a new 'seriously rich' 'overclass' (Walker 1990). By the mid-1990s there was a consensus of middle ground opinion that the very visible wrongs suffered by young people outcast from housing and labour markets could best be averted in the future by giving families better economic support (Young and Halsey 1995), and by providing all young people with worthwhile jobs (Dahrendorf *et al.* 1995). This and similar thinking has already produced several imaginative blueprints for future economic and social policy. In the meantime, what about *today's* poor? What can be done to redress the wrongs already suffered by the cohorts of 1990s excluded youth, those who during the Thatcher years left school and went straight into unemployment, homelessness and destitution? How feasible is it to expect these alienated young citizens to return to the 'family' and exploitative occupational structures which, as they themselves might put it, they have already 'sacked'?

Modernist certainties and postmodern implosions

From the seventeenth century onwards the official approach to poverty has been shaped and infused by a modernist optimism that through schooling, work, familiness and the penal system the poor can be kept in their place. At the same time, this modernist faith in a governmentality based on manifestations of organized self-interest has always been shot through with premodernist fears about the uncontainable poor – just one threatening sector from a whole array of deviants (mystics, artists, comedians, criminals, radicals and revolutionaries in the arts and sciences) whose irrepressible and refractory existences have continually bucked modernist systems and made postmodernism always and already possible.

Towards the end of the nineteenth century thousands of working-class children were swept into industrial schools and reformatories. At the beginning of the twentieth century, the young street children were rounded up and corralled in the 'child saving' institutions. Then, as the century progressed, things seemed to get better, especially for a brief period in postwar Britain. 1950s children, nourished by their welfare orange juice and free school milk, were told stories of the 'bad old days' when youngsters from poverty-stricken homes ran the streets in bare feet while older siblings queued at soup kitchens for the family's food and other doles. But these were Dickensian fables for a winter's night, and it was complacently assumed that they were only of historical interest now that the era of the welfare state had dawned. The message was that those hard times could not come again and, for the majority of young persons leaving school during the short-lived consumer boom of the 1960s, it did indeed seem that welfare capitalism had 'delivered'. Not so. Even by the late 1960s the cracks were showing – in the form of increased youth homelessness and persisting poverty. When, a decade later, Prime Minister Thatcher decided that a return to Victorian values would provide the most appropriate ped-agogy for the nation's (poorer) youth, the return also of barefoot young people to urban streets, and the resurrection of the 'soup kitchen' (at first in the poorer parts of towns, but later right in the central shopping areas) were not long delayed.

However, the expectations of 1980s youth were both much higher than, and qualitatively different to, those of the young poor of previous eras. Moreover, as young people became poorer and poorer, images of their own possible and impossible existences were continuously and teasingly refracted in multimedia representations of what it is to be poor and young in 'today's informationalised, yet more than ever capitalist world order' (Lash 1994: 110).

For some, the celebration of youth 'difference' took on global dimensions as they participated in internationalized music, fashion and drug cultures – though the risks of such participation were inevitably borne disproportionately by the destitute young least able to fund the new consumerist lifestyles by legitimate means. With the rundown of welfare, the casualties amongst those playing for high stakes in fashionable consumption gambles (whether the 'prizes' were houses or drugs) received little mercy. They were swiftly evicted from homes (for not paying the mortgage) or expelled from schools (for drugtaking) – both punishments serving as warnings to the 'others'. Yet, although fears of a growing and threatening underclass were frenetically fuelled by a rabid press, the dominant scenario of the 1980s – the unbridled and predatory pursuit of individual wealth – was always enacted against a backcloth of principled (though fragmented) dissent.

In the couple of decades prior to 1979, several new politically conscious groupings had emerged: for instance, the women's movement, celebrating a variety of feminisms; the anti-racist movement, promoting anti-racist policies in all areas of public life; and the gay rights movement, fighting against all forms of discrimination propagated on the grounds of sexual orientation. Each of these resisted Thatcher's attempts to turn back the cultural clock to Victorian times and, with the New Right itself vigorously promoting a radical and deregulationist individualism, many of the old certainties of both Right and Left began to implode.

Meanwhile, a constituency of resistance to the punishing inequities being piled on the already-poor – though not a politically articulated or self-conscious resistance – gradually coalesced from within the ranks of the newly-outcast young. A significant number of youngsters, having been brought up to expect that citizenship should reside in social rights rather than property rights, resisted punitive attempts to fob them off with meaningless jobs, store them away in state institutions, or force them to live with families wherein they had been sexually or physically abused; or where poverty-induced conflict was making their lives unbearable. Concomitantly, the rampant consumerism which was a major element in Thatcherite populism made it unlikely that these new destitute young would settle for a deferential approach towards penny-pinching welfare bureaucracies. Instead, some took what might be called a more participatory, or even combative, stance towards 'welfare'. Turning their backs on the families and other traditional 'authorities' that had so badly let them down, they set about making their own lives, and in doing so, they attempted to transform themselves from victims into survivors.

Survivalism is a main theme of this book. None the less, in the following pages it should soon become apparent that the individualistic ethic of survivalism (which is, after all, the flip side of unfettered economic competition) can never be the basis of either a social ethic or even (long-term) survival. The young people who speak in this book had reason to be only too well aware of that – and a majority of them were. Yet they, and other young adults who have struggled to develop new ways of coping with old problems (and whose pleasures and pains seem to be equally incomprehensible to large sectors of the already 'included' majority), are unlikely to acquiesce in governmental and political plans to 'define' them in (as proposed by Dahrendorf 1985), unless their own views and new ways of living are taken seriously. Rather than being merely 'defined in', today's presently outcast youth must be allowed to 'define themselves in'. The ethnographic materials presented in later chapters of this book make it very clear that, as attempts are made to repair the damage of the Thatcher years, it will not be enough to woo (or coerce) the young survivor/victims of those years by offering them stakes in what they have already rejected. Additionally, and more radically, their new ways of living outwith 'the family' will need to be legitimated and supported; some of their presently criminalized lifestyles and pleasures – such as New Age travelling and cannabis use – will need to be legalized; and new and more democratic modes of state-obligated social and criminal justice will have to be realized.

Author's main arguments

Since the mid-nineteenth century, the meanings of youth homelessness have been variably activated within and outwith three of the state's principal modes of governance: *discipline* (of youth); *legal and technobureaucratic control* (of the homelessness state); and *ideological accommodation* (of threats to both state legitimacy and the ontological well-being of individuals).

The *protocols* for the governance of youth homelessness that have surfaced (often simultaneously) at different times and places can be characterized as being: premodern, insofar as they draw on primitive fears of disease, contamination and the mysterious powers of 'otherness'; modernist insofar as they seek damage limitation via regimes of deterrence, denial and discipline; and postmodernist insofar as they can both empower and disempower according to the prevailing political and ideological conditions within which youth regimes and youth identities are fashioned, fragmented and refracted differentially – not only by all those who are 'homeless' but also by all those who are 'at home' in Britain today.

The two dominant *discourses* within which the political meanings of homelessness have been constituted from the days of 'vagabondage' right through to the era of the 'underclass' have been those of *'less eligibility'* and *'citizen risk'*.

Despite its archival palimpsestry, contemporary youth homelessness is very much a twentieth-century production. Its specificity inheres, on the one hand, in the state's fine-tuning of its ideological accommodation of homelessness. On the other, it inheres in the reflexive consciousness of today's homeless youth (a consciousness enhanced and refracted daily by mass media reporting on homelessness and 'underclass' exotica) that they have been outcast from both housing and labour markets.

A significant number of homeless young adults have had their otherwise mundane worlds so violently fractured by the effects of affordable housing scarcity, unemployment and cuts in welfare provision, that their attempts to survive and repair their shattered lives *necessarily* involve a reordering of political, moral and economic possibilities. Such reordering produces new modalities of living that are usually mundane, sometimes exotic and often crimogenic. Amongst the most destitute of the young homeless a culture of *survivalism* develops.

One prerequisite to an ethical and political understanding of the crimes of outcast youth is an understanding of both prevailing asymmetries of citizenship and the *anti*-social controls which those asymmetries perpetuate.

The most striking feature of the relationship between youth homelessness and crime as suggested by the young homeless narrators in the Three Cities Project was that while a majority of them had been victims of crimes whose perpetrators would never be punished, whenever they themselves had been seen to deviate – from social mores, respectability, or the criminal law – they had received punishments of a magnitude out of all proportion to their initial wrongdoing.

The jigsaw

The first two chapters of the book describe the historical production and contemporary governance of youth homelessness. Chapters 3 and 4 provide ethnographic descriptions of the endeavours of the homeless young as they strive to make new lives for themselves in a variety of settings. The illustrative materials are all taken from two empirical studies of youth homelessness directed by the author in the early 1990s, and referred to throughout as the Three Cities Project (Carlen 1995b) and the Shropshire Project (Carlen and Wardhaugh 1992).

The presentational (anti-structural) method of *Jigsaw* was developed with the twofold aim of avoiding a positivistic presentation of ethnographic data at the same time as developing a strong argument about the relationships between crime, politics and youth homelessness. The search for such a method was prompted by a number of reservations about the focus and method of the Three Cities Project, as well as by a growing dissatisfaction with both traditional criminology's 'search for a paradigm' (Carlen 1996) and traditional ethnography's narrative approach. This latter, despite its commitment to naturalism (i.e. to tell it like it is), too often erases ambiguities and contradictions, conflates answers to entirely different questions, and ties up loose ends in the service of narrative coherence. At other times it demolishes whole histories, biographies and stories in the service of 'case' construction. In social policy research there is the additional temptation to reduce and simplify by constructing taxonomies of culpability or need (cf. Wood 1985).

As far as the Three Cities Project was concerned, there were, from the outset, doubts about the propriety of designing an investigation which might imply *causal* links between homelessness and crime; the fear was that any focus on crime and policing in the interviews might inevitably assign lawbreaking an importance that it does not have in the lives of young homeless people.

That being so, it may have been unfortunate that the grant application for the award which funded the Three Cities Project was entitled 'Young people, lawbreaking, criminalization and homelessness in Manchester, Birmingham and Stoke-on-Trent'. It certainly provoked hostility from reviewers who thought it implied that all homeless people are more than likely to be predisposed towards lawbreaking! Yet, despite appearances, the research proposal presumed no such thing. Given that definitions of homelessness are so broad, it would obviously have been impossible to set up any kind of meaningful research to find out 'how many homeless people commit crime', or 'whether homelessness causes crime'. It was neither assumed that the majority of homeless people become lawbreakers, nor that homelessness 'causes' crime in any mechanistic or deterministic sense.

What *was* already known from numerous sources was: that many young people who are homeless also experience some trouble with the police; that from 1989 many more young people than in previous years had no visible means of support; that homelessness is a dominant factor in reoffending; and that young people on the run often elect to break the law in order either to live in the style of their choice or under circumstances over which they feel they have no control.

It was therefore proposed to interview 100 presently homeless young persons between the ages of 16 and 30 in three cities in central England to find out just how they do manage to live once they are without a secure home and, in many cases, also without any visible or sufficient means of support. During the period prior to the commencement of that research an opportunity was offered to conduct a homelessness survey of young persons in predominantly rural Shropshire, and 50 homeless young people were interviewed in that county (Carlen and Wardhaugh 1992).

In neither project did the interviews focus on crime to the exclusion of other issues about homeless life-histories and lifestyles. In some stories law-breaking hardly featured at all; in others there was much talk about what a lawyer or a criminologist would most probably call crime but what in the young people's narratives featured as descriptions of normal parental behaviour. The stories recounted later in this book have been chosen to illustrate these aspects of the interviewees' accounts.

However, David Wagner's splendid study (Wagner 1993) of a homeless community in the United States makes trenchant criticisms of this type of one-time interview method of social investigation, which so frequently portrays street life as pathological. Wagner's main criticism of the one-time interview method is that by interviewing people only once, and when they are in crisis, researchers miss out on the ways in which people help themselves and others to emerge from crises and go on to develop community and political action informed by reflections on their own homelessness experience. More provocatively, Wagner (1993: 8) asserts that, 'A second reason for the findings of vulnerability, disaffiliation, and pathology involves the professional training of researchers, advocates and social service providers'. Yet, although Wagner's contention that a one-off interview must necessarily deny interviewees a past and a future does itself deny to them the capacity to remember and recall, his abhorrence of sociological accounts which pathologize social action is in the best (Durkheimian) sociological tradition. Nevertheless, Wagner's stance simplifies some of the complexities inherent both in empirical research and in the relation of a writer's own values to the final report.

The first issue in relation to a researcher's own values and/or interests is pinpointed by the question, 'Why study homelessness?' If homeless people and homelessness are unremarkable in any way, why bother to investigate them and it? My own answer is that to have so many young people suffering the extremes of pain and destitution that youth homelessness engenders is an undesirable state of affairs.

Methodologically, the more important point is that it is desirable in any political and qualitative analysis of interview transcripts to distinguish between the political conditions that engender a widespread youth homelessness, and the way in which that homelessness state has multiple and diverse meanings for the people who, in occupying it (for longer or shorter periods, through 'choice' or not) become known as 'the homeless'.

Similarly, just as the concepts of homelessness and the homeless should not be conflated, neither are the sociological dualities of agency/structure, victim/survivor, or normal/pathological very useful in analysing the extremely complex and contradictory meanings conferred on the term homelessness by those who either experience or witness it. For example: although all of the respondents who had left home or run away from local authority care thought that in the circumstances they had done the right thing, they none the less talked reflexively and at length about the unexpected 'paranoia' which they felt had been provoked by street and/or hostel life, of their powerlessness in confrontations with the various bureaucracies, and of their desire for a better life.

Likewise, although the young people's courage, resilience, organization and the analytical way in which the majority of them talked about themselves, their pasts and their hoped-for futures was very impressive, sombre reflection on the economic and political conditions which facilitated their states of homelessness (see Chapters 1 and 2) suggests that having the will to survive is, in itself, not sufficient to lift them out of their present less-than-desirable circumstances. Indeed, it is *because* their identities have been moulded in the interstices between historical and contemporary conditions of existence that those identities are, at one and the same time, both possible and impossible, both plausible and implausible.

Finally, although analyses of the links between homelessness and crime indicate that lawbreaking by homeless people is but a very minor aspect of the totality of relationships between (anti) social controls, lawbreaking, criminalization and youth homelessness, they also suggest (to me, at least, but also to some of those interviewed) that by committing crime young people already in poverty provoke the further disempowerment of both themselves and their similarly destitute victims.

In relation, therefore, to this last clutch of contradictions, the jigsaw method has yet another function: to illuminate some of the disjunctions in the picturing of homelessness states and identities as they are pictured in Chapters 3 and 4 by previously delineating (in Chapters 1 and 2) the historical and contemporary conditions which makes those depictions both possible and impossible, both plausible and implausible.

So . . . it is for all those very complex reasons that this book has been constituted by the jigsaw method, a mixed-mode of analytic description, argument and counter-argument which, rather than trying to impose a very strong narrative coherence on the whole text, merely pieces together fragments of narrative in such a way as to suggest all kinds of homelessness cameos which, taken together, may be contradictory and raise more issues than they resolve. For although I hope that what follows will present youth homelessness in some new lights, the aim of the jigsaw method is to convince readers that there is no one definitive story to be told. Sure, *I* choose to tell a particular tale – and it's a different one to Wagner's. But I hope that it contains sufficient clues to help readers understand both why the story takes the form it does and why, also, it can never capture the lived experiences of homeless people in all the fullness of their contradictions. It is, therefore, the distinct aim of the jigsaw method of presentation to self-destruct, to provide enough pieces from the empirical archive to predestine its picture to be unceasingly wrenched from the frame and put together differently. *If* that happens, the Jigsaw will have achieved at least one of its aims.

1 |

THE PRODUCTION OF
YOUTH HOMELESSNESS

Homelessness and the homeless are twentieth-century productions. Vagabondage, vagrancy, paupers, tramps, hoboes, dossers, gypsies, travellers, the houseless, slum-dwellers, streetchildren, and the omnipresent poor pre-existed them, but it took the failed liberal-democratic welfare states of the twentieth century to create homelessness as a finely-tuned, bureaucratic instrument for defining, indexing, redeploying, normalizing and abnormalizing the young, unemployed homeless as one welfare class too many. And, in the long and intricate journey from vagabondage through various forms and degrees of houselessness to homelessness, and then youth homelessness, the two dominant discourses repeatedly subsuming all others (for example, moral desert, beneficence, need, citizen rights, economic growth, philanthropy, state obligation and state legitimacy) are those of *less eligibility* and *citizen risk*.

Yet the poor and the homeless have survived. The stories of those survivals are what this book is about. Integral to their telling is an intricate narrative jigsaw, pieces of which are hijacked from other sociopolitical histories – of employment, unemployment, penality, welfare, housing reform, childhood, youth and family. None of the bits really fit together. That's the difficulty. *R*edressing homelessness always involves *ad*dressing homelessness – and the latter is a contradiction in terms. The proffered collage with its gaps and overlaps therefore traces only a partial knowledge of the meanings, metaphors and metonymies of homelessness at the end of the twentieth century. There is always an Other story. Knowing it and not knowing it is why attempts to confront homelessness usually make for a certain uneasiness.

Vagabonds and vagrants

Before the fifteenth century had run its course, a number of factors, ranging from the social upheavals following the Black Death to the disruptions caused by the Wars of the Roses, had combined to produce a class of itinerant beggars.

(Pound 1971: 3)

The terms vagabond and vagrant have been around since the mid-fifteenth century, but although all dictionary definitions include itinerancy as a key element in both concepts, the primary concern of the Vagrancy Act of 1598 was not that itinerant beggars were without *shelter* but that, being without regular work, they were also without *masters*; that is, they were masterless men. Discourses on indigency, however, were as complex and contradictory in early-modern as in late-modern times and the exact balancing and prioritizing of them in ideologies and policies is difficult to assess.

> The condition of poverty was not yet understood solely in economic terms . . . For Catholics as well as Protestants the life and example of Christ was still an important guideline in the perception of social order . . . Things were, however, no longer as simple as in the Middle Ages, when the poor were predominantly seen as a means of salvation for the rich. The latter were required by the church to act charitably, while in return the poor were obliged to pray for the soul of the alms-giver. Even some decades before the Reformation a far-reaching change can be noticed: since then the poor had been considered both blessed and condemned by God, virtuous and sinful, industrious and lazy . . .
>
> Not for the Church, but for early modern governments and magistrates, the poor were mainly a problem of public order, and only to a lesser extent public relief.
>
> (Jutte 1994: 194–5)

Moreover, and as Slack (1990) points out, the thesis that regulation of the poor in the sixteenth and seventeenth centuries was related solely to control of the surplus labour force, has to be set against evidence that close surveillance and spatial control of mendicancy continued even during times of labour scarcity. For then as now, the strategic incentives for the governance of homelessness were the management of social change and the maintenance of public order . . . but always with an eye to the price that the taxpaying electorate would be willing to pay.

By the first half of the sixteenth century most European towns had centralized bureaucracies for the administration of poor relief. Concomitantly, local bureaucrats were already being faced with the related problems of definition and entitlement that are inherent in dole systems and which have perennially plagued welfare managers since Elizabethan times (Slack 1990; Jutte 1994).

Throughout the sixteenth and seventeenth centuries vagrancy was predominantly a young person's crime. Punishments were deterrent (offenders were whipped), while the regulatory measure of returning vagrants to their 'parishes of settlement' was aimed at keeping down the taxes of an unwilling host neighbourhood. (It also contributed to an increase in accommodation scarcity as landowners engaged in a massive demolition of cottages in order to avoid the settlement of immigrant labour to whom they would have a 'chargeable liability' (Burnett 1978: 37). Woman-headed

households were not unusual, though Slack implies that single mother-
hood was as threatening to the first Elizabethans as to their namesakes of
the twentieth century, observing that the poor law statutes of 1598 and
1601 were 'passed at a time when the problem of poverty was unusually
severe'; illegitimacy rates were at a peak, and 'probably levels of crime and
vagrancy also'. 'It is not difficult', he concludes, 'to see why poverty seemed
a threat and improved policing a necessary response' (Slack 1990: 11–12).

At the same time, it has to be acknowledged that Christian humanistic
discourses had had some currency in England from the mid-sixteenth
century. These continued to manifest themselves throughout the seventeenth and eighteenth centuries. Their most tangible influence can be seen
in the philosophy behind the early workhouses which (unlike those of the
nineteenth century based on deterrence and/or discipline), were inspired
by a Renaissance optimism engendering belief that governments could successfully engage in the social engineering which would eventually elimi-
nate poverty through moral reform (Slack 1990: 14). None the less, and
even though a distinction had been drawn between the deserving and the
undeserving poor from the late Middle Ages onwards, Karel Williams
(1981) convincingly argues that right up until the Poor Law Amendment
Act of 1834 extensive outdoor relief was given to unemployed able-bodied
men.

As costs had risen, however, there had been increased criticism of the
failure of local poor law overseers to distinguish between *entitlement* (on
the grounds of a welfare applicant's need) and *desert* (on the grounds of an
impotent pauper's genuine inability to work). Consequently, and in
response to ever more urgent calls to cut the costs of statutory poor relief,
the 1834 Poor Law (Amendment) Act enshrined the principle of *less eligibility* in punitive legislation designed to ensure that able-bodied men and
their families were thenceforth ineligible for the outdoor relief popularly
assumed to make them better-off than labourers in paid employment.
Under the Act, the able-bodied and their families were to be sent to workhouses where they would be subjected to a discipline fashioned to 'repel
the indolent and the vicious' (Webb and Webb 1910: 10). But still the major
social problem was seen to be *lack of work* rather than *lack of shelter*, and,
although the 1834 legislation refers to the 'houseless poor', it was only
when the *urban poor* began to be seen as a major blot on the industrial landscape that the spotlight was turned on *housing*.

Slums and housing reforms

> The cottage-homes of England
> How beautiful they smell.
> There's fever in the cesspool
> And sewage in the well.
> (*Punch*, 23 May 1834 in Rubinstein 1974)

By the middle of the nineteenth century, governments, and the middle and upper classes, were beginning to accept that it was in their own interests to do something about appalling housing conditions. Rapid population growth in the newly industrialized manufacturing centres, as the already-dispossessed from rural areas flocked to the towns in search of work, together with the miasmic theory of contagion which led the better-off to fear that the diseases of the urban slums would eventually penetrate their own drawing rooms and kill them all off, lent urgency to finding new ways of picturing the 'problem of the poor', and for a time the question of welfare in general was dominated by 'The Housing Question'. All the old beliefs about less eligibility, desert, and cost persisted, however, and progress was slow. Additionally, a new element of plebiphobia entered destitution discourses as rate and taxpayers, reluctant to cough up more funds for poor relief, argued that people who lived like pigs did so through choice, and that, therefore, money spent on the provision of decent housing for them would be money wasted. As Enid Gauldie (1974: 27) comments: 'it ["the pigsty theory"] was a strong and perennial argument, and it turned up again as the "coals in the bath" theory of the twentieth century'.

Accordingly, even though with the passing of The Lodging Houses Act (later known as Shaftsbury's Act), 'council house building and the assumption of state responsibility for the housing of the poor became legislatively possible in 1851' (Gauldie 1974: 239) and despite the proliferation of housing legislation during the rest of the century, the only material housing benefits to accrue to the nineteenth-century poor were those emanating from the model dwellings built by various mill and factory owners (such as Robert Owen and George Cadbury) or large landowners (like the Duke of Bedford) for their (by definition 'deserving') *workers*. Slum clearance activity in itself merely squeezed newly-displaced inhabitants into the less visible flop houses of adjoining rookeries, while there was no shortage of enterprising builders eager to 'in-fill' any gaps between already-overflowing tenements (Marr 1904: 85; London County Council 1913: 22).

The destitute unemployed requiring alms or shelter had to demonstrate need by putting themselves in the workhouse, an option that after 1834 most men either with or without families would avoid if they could (see Twining 1898). The workhouses were finally abolished by The National Assistance Act 1948, though campaigners on behalf of the homeless claimed that the 'workhouse mentality' continued to shape the attitudes and practices of the welfare authorities charged under the same Act with providing emergency accommodation for homeless families (Bailey 1973). Similar accusations can still be heard on the eve of the twenty-first century.

About the same time that it was recognized that *poverty* rather than lack of sanitation was the chief cause of slum conditions, so too it gradually dawned on a bourgeoisie still easily frightened by the spectres of King Cholera and Revolution that

It was the presence in towns of a large body of people living without
any wages at all which caused the housing problem in the first place
and allowed it to grow to unmanageable proportions.

(Gauldie, 1974: 153)

Something must be done, but not yet – and preferably as cheaply as possible! It was to take one war (1914–18) to provide the spur to any really significant house-building by local councils ('of all new houses built between
1890 and 1914 less than 5 per cent were provided by local authorities';
Burnett 1978: 181); and a second (1939–1945) before any comprehensive
attack on poverty itself was mounted.

No place like home

A major function of the charitable societies of the late nineteenth century
was the transmission to the respectable working-class recipients of their
ministrations and alms of a belief in self and social betterment through
rational budgeting and the wholesome use of leisure. In future, respectable
working-class pastimes should be pursued in domestic or institutional
privacy rather than in public space, and those which did occur in public
should be organized rather than spontaneous. The respectable home
should be a sanctuary from worldly temptations and a shrine to virtue and
the sanctity of family life (see Burnett 1978: 193). This emphasis on
respectability was maintained in the deferential model of scientific charity
propagated by reformers like Octavia Hill (1875) and the Charity Organization Society; through the more participatory models advocated by the
practical socialism of the Settlement movement which aimed to break
down the cultural barriers between classes; to the statist model of social
security aspired to by the postwar welfare state (see Garland 1985 for a
detailed analysis of the interweaving of penal and welfare discourses in the
early 1900s). On the whole, though, Daunton (1983: 272) argues,

> It would be wrong . . . to interpret the changed attitude towards con-
> sumption, leisure and the use of the public domain simply in terms of
> an imposition from above. Rising real wages and greater regularity of
> employment provided the incentive to readjust patterns of consump-
> tion. The intensification of regulation over the workplace increased
> the attraction of a shift away from a culture based upon the workplace
> to a culture based upon the home and family. Indeed, many members
> of the working class welcomed and accepted the sterilization of public
> space, and switched to an expenditure pattern which entailed a more
> inward-looking life style. *The respectable working man would argue that*
> *the streets were for those who did not have a decent home.* (italics added)

Thus, while men of the dangerous classes were left to beat up and sexually terrorize their wives and children on the streets, the respectables of the

working and other classes would continue to engage in the same activities in the privacy of the home (Pizzey 1974; Dobash and Dobash 1979). The Englishman's home was not only his castle, it was even seen by some of the opponents of state housing provision as being symbolic of his independence and masculinity. Note, for instance, the words of a leading town clerk who, in the 1920s, asserted that 'Ever since the days of the cave man, man has provided the house for his women!' (quoted in Simon 1929: 75).

There was still particular concern about 'street urchins', young beggars and child prostitutes, though it was their poverty rather than their law-breaking that made working-class children prime candidates for incarceration in industrial schools and reformatories. By 1894 17,000 children were held in industrial schools and 1400 in reformatories (Morris *et al.* 1980). Yet as late as the 1880s it was estimated that, in London alone, there were over 30,000 homeless youngsters sleeping rough, staying in casual wards or lodging in unregistered houses (Hutson and Liddiard 1994: 2, quoting statistics from Rose 1988: 136). Gradually, however,

> The introduction of compulsory education ... and the dwindling opportunities for child labour took children off the streets. In the 'Children's Charter' of 1908, parents could be punished for causing their children to beg and these children could be put in orphanages. At the same time, the National Society for the Prevention of Cruelty to Children (NSPCC) and workhouse authorities removed the children who were travelling with itinerant adults.
>
> (Hutson and Liddiard 1994: 2)

Thus were the offspring of the very poor systematically rounded up and corralled *en masse* in institutions, the 'Homes' wherein many of them, and their children in turn, were to be variously abused, neglected or forgotten during the course of the twentieth century.

The Great Privatization of family life, already in progress during the eleventh century, when the lords and ladies of the castles partitioned themselves off from their retainers, had now reached the working classes. Increasingly, they were persuaded that it would be politic to shun as dangerous all those who, spurning home and hearth, spent inordinate amounts of time in public places of ill-repute, and/or, worse, were of no fixed abode.

At the neighbourhood level, lines of class demarcation had been integral to industrial urban development. In 1845, Engels (1969) tellingly noted of 1840s Manchester that middle-class people could quickly pass through working-class districts 'without ever seeing the ... misery and grime which forms the complement of their wealth' (quoted in Bentley 1981: 56). To avoid altogether the pollution of the city and the 'dangerous poor', aspiring artisans now attempted to achieve an almost complete segregation by joining the 'Dunroaminers' in the new working-class suburbs (see Burnett 1978; Bentley 1981). 'No Hawkers' notices were fixed to garden gates, and for several decades residents lived window to window rather than face to face.

Then, in the late 1980s, the wheel came full circle; suffering another 'fear of crime' wave, the more energetic suburbanites temporarily achieved an hitherto absent sense of community by joining Neighbourhood Watch groups formed especially to keep under surveillance any strangers seen wandering around their middle-class enclaves (see Hope 1995 for an overview of community crime prevention schemes). At last the irony had been brought home; that as Christopher Stanley (1995) puts it,

> the urban public sphere has always included contradictory elements of liminality (heterotopias) . . . Modernity is founded on generalising the rationalised, economic space of the market to other urban spaces as the public sphere. One aspect of this dissemination of the economic to other spaces of economic life is that social exchange with strangers is no less set aside from the everyday but becomes a constituent element of the everyday, we are all strangers and nomads . . . In the metropolis nobody is an outsider, but, then, nobody is an insider either.

Depictions of beggars, vagrants and vagabonds as fraudulent rogues had been abroad since medieval times (see Thomas 1932). At the beginning of the twentieth century, as the availability of regular employment increased while that of casual work declined, this age-old phobia was aggravated by exaggerated accounts of the wildness of gangs of road and railway builders (navvies) and the insurrectionary potential of dockers. Anxieties about the safety of property, the respectability of neighbourhoods, and the realization of property values all mixed together and occasioned a renewed fear of itinerancy. To this day, that fear of personified threats to property values has periodically manifested itself in persecutory activities against New Age travellers, gypsies, caravan and 'homeless hostel' dwellers, and casual workers whose employment takes them away from home. Furthermore, the relentless reiteration of the fiction that *Irish* immigrant labour was especially responsible for the growth of slum housing engendered yet one more justification for a racist discrimination against *all* immigrant workers (especially in the area of housing) which is still prevalent today. Stedman Jones (1971) has provided a detailed account of how this stigmatization of the casual poor was a product of the combined but differing interests of the middle classes, artisans *and* the emergent labour movement.

Many regular workers, having a greater attachment to locality than to domesticity (and to putting their hard-earned money into their own pockets rather than into those of the landlord or rent-collector), refused to move into the better housing for which, being in work, they were deemed eligible (see Simon 1929: 55). Nor were all of the 'incorrigible' poor rounded up and incarcerated. Various undomiciled undesirables stayed at large, scavenging in the alleys and courts of the still-rancid slums. Others dossed under the railway arches as down and outs; or travelled the roads as casual labourers, tramps and tinkers. For while conservatives continued to think that having a home was a sign of respectability and, for a married man, proof of masculine probity, *not* being in a *Home* (state institution) was, as the twentieth century wore on, increasingly seen by children in (or previously in) state care as being a badge of independence (see for instance Carlen *et al.* 1985; Carlen 1988). Indeed, fear of institutional abuse at the hands of state welfare (experienced by the most vulnerable of the poor since the workhouse era) has arguably been of greater significance in the production of 1990's runaways than it was in the histories of 1890's street urchins. It should also be noted that, by the 1980s, it was increasingly being accepted that many children run away from the family home because they have suffered sexual abuse there. Those stories will be told later. Here, the chronicle moves on to Beveridge and the post-1945 settlement between labour and capital.

Welfare state?

The aspirations of Lloyd-George's wartime coalition government to build a land fit for heroes to return to remained an unrealized ideal – so much so that wags were subsequently provoked to comment that you had to *be* a hero to survive the unemployment and overcrowded housing conditions in the England of the 1920s and 1930s. 'The housing experience of many people', John Burnett (1978: 304) argues, showed little major change until,

> in the years after World War II, a period of rapid house building, both public and private, coincided with full employment and a rising standard of living to produce an effective demand.

It also coincided with the new era of welfare regulation that from 1945 onwards propagated, with missionary vigour, the ideology of family and home as twin cornerstones of the decent society – as thenceforth to be realized via the welfare state. The subsequent use of social-work pedagogy to school whole families in the virtues of self-governance as part of the welfare deal is described in the next chapter. In this chapter, the focus remains on the *production* of homelessness, though, as will be seen (and has already been noted in the context of the old Poor Law), the legal and bureaucratic apparatuses established to limit or decrease homelessness have too often been simultaneously implicated in its production and reproduction. Be that as it may, by the time postwar governments were attempting to deliver the nation from Want by implementing the National Insurance scheme proposed by Beveridge (1942), the assumptions behind his report were already at odds with the aspirations and age structure of a rapidly changing society.

Both the Beveridge Report and local council housing policies were based on the assumption that the major unit of consumption to be targeted for the delivery of state welfare and housing provision was the nuclear family, headed by one main (and male) breadwinner, and moreover, that grown-up children (including newly-weds) would live with their parents until such time as they could obtain their own home. A combination of changed circumstances, however, resulted in young married couples being no longer prepared to lodge in the parental home even for a short time: they were marrying at a younger age than their parents had; they entertained higher standard-of-living expectations than had been held by previous generations of working people; and, because full employment had enabled them to take advantage of the late 1950s consumer boom, they had many more material goods to house. Decisively, too, the obsessive privatization of family life had continued apace.

Unfortunately, and despite the massive building and rebuilding programmes undertaken by Aneurin Bevan (Labour Minister of Health and Housing, 1945–51) and Harold Macmillan (Conservative Minister of Housing and Local Government 1951–4), the supply of housing still fell short of demand. Worse, the residual effects of war damage, the demolition of unfit dwellings under the slum clearance programmes (restarted in 1954), the continuing decrease in the availability of privately rented accommodation, plus the increase in demand for independent housing for single people all resulted in it being apparent by 1960 'that a new housing crisis was looming. In particular, much publicity was given to the growing problem of homelessness' (Burnett 1978: 278). Six years later the National Assistance Board (1966) published its report, *Homeless Single Persons*. It found that 102 (11.6 per cent) of 743 men discovered sleeping rough in a nation-wide count on 6 December 1965 had been under the age of 30, while only 2450 (10 per cent) of the 25,490 men surveyed in the lodging-houses and hostels had been under the same age. The report therefore concluded that,

> The information obtained during the Survey about the age of people using Centres and the age of people found sleeping rough and also about the period over which they had been using Centres or sleeping rough does not suggest that an increasing number of young people are taking up this way of life permanently. Amongst the younger men it seemed that many slept rough or had been using Centres on one occasion only or for a short while, for a particular reason or in a particular situation. It was among the older men that it had tended to become more a way of life.
>
> (National Assistance Board 1966: 172)

Portents of the futures of homelessness were, none the less, already on the horizon:

> the information about age might seem to suggest that the size of the problem will decline. However, among those using Reception Centres, many said they had started leading an unsettled life following a disturbance in personal relationships, such as the breakdown of a marriage or the death of a parent or wife.
>
> (National Assistance Board 1966: 172)

Predictably, in less than a decade, a new national study was finding both that young people were overrepresented in the homeless population (Drake *et al.* 1981: 20) and that there appeared to be more homeless women than had shown up in previous research. Even more importantly, an entirely new factor in the production of homelessness was being stressed: 'problems of access to and scarcity of housing for single people' (Drake *et al.* 1981: 9). Disappointingly, young single people had not been made a priority category in the 1977 Housing (Homeless Persons) Act, and by 1986 it was being estimated that there were 180,000 single homeless in Britain and that homelessness was growing fastest among young people (Greve 1991). In December 1994, the homelessness campaigning group Shelter reported that although

> There are no comprehensive statistics for single homelessness nation-ally . . . In London alone the London Association of London Authori-ties (ALA) and Single Homelessness in London (SHIL) have estimated that there are 140,000 single homeless people.
>
> (Shelter 1994a)

In February 1995, an analysis of research on inequality of income in the UK revealed that incomes had rapidly become less equal during the 1980s and that the real wages of the lowest paid young workers were below those of their immediate predecessors (Barclay 1995: 13–20). How did the brave new world of postwar welfare capitalism degenerate into the socially polarized 1990s?

State welfare and the politics of Thatcherism

To get any kind of grasp on the politics of youth and youth homelessness in Britain under the Thatcher and post-Thatcher Conservative govern-ments, it is necessary to take a closer look at the type of welfare state which Margaret Thatcher's first administration inherited in 1979. Furthermore, to facilitate even a partial understanding of the texture and career of welfare statism in Britain, it will first be useful to ponder again on the mixed traditions of British philanthropy, and in particular, on the kind of poor relief available in Britain immediately prior to the 1834 Poor Law (Amend-ment) Act.

Welfare state regimes have all (to a greater or lesser extent) been predi-cated upon a recognition that, left to themselves, market forces do not always create the best conditions for the reproduction of capitalist states, and that therefore a certain level of intervention is required in order to regulate class relations. Programmes of intervention which give people access to certain social goods independently of market forces concomi-tantly both reduce the recipients' degree of commodification and endow them with social rights. Karl Polyani (1944, referred to in Esping-Andersen 1990: 36) claims that, prior to the 1834 Poor Law (Amendment) Act, the

Speenham-land System of allowing outdoor relief to the unemployed had shielded British labourers from the complete commodification by market forces which, immediately after 1834, either forced the able-bodied unemployed into the mill towns in search of work, or into the workhouses for official pauperization. However, and as Paul Slack (1990: 55) points out, it is at least arguable that the system of relief prior to 1834 had not only raised people's expectations about what constituted an adequate standard of living, but also ensured that definitions of poverty were kept on the political agenda, even at times when living standards were rising. Thus, although the scientific charity model of the later nineteenth-century Charity Organization Society housing schemes was explicitly shaped by traditional Poor Law principles of liberal (Protestant) self-reliance and moral desert, mixed with recent Malthusian notions about the pauperization effects of public relief, the more participatory models of charity implicit in early twentieth-century practical socialism could tap into an already embryonic participatory tradition of local poor relief.

Prior to 1834, a system of needs-based doles had led people to develop expectations of welfare as a right. Subsequently the liberal Protestant principle of less eligibility, which has manifested itself in successive British welfare schemes, has also been regularly challenged and subverted by a fraction of genuinely eligible claimants whose folk traditions have taught them that they must themselves develop a degree of rule manipulation if they wish to beat the welfare bureaucrats at their official and archival games of desert evaluation and risk assessment. The omnipresent liberal capitalist state in Britain has never given anything away except under threat of war, riot or debility. Moreover, full commitment to the decommodification of labour was achieved neither by the Keynesian interventionism of the 1930s nor by the postwar neo-Keynesian welfare state. Instead, the British welfare state's brief (but decisive) flowering during the 1945–50 Labour government was suddenly brought to an end by fierce competition from abroad. A series of financial crises followed, and after

the balance of payments crisis of 1965–66 . . . [trade union] resistance to forced cuts in living standards led to poor industrial relations being perceived as the root of the British problem.

The Tory government elected in 1970 was committed to a radical programme of economic reform which foreshadowed what was to come in 1979.

(Brake and Hale 1992: 4)

By the time Margaret Thatcher came to power as prime minister in 1979, the outgoing Labour government had already tried to control social spending by making cutbacks in education and housing, economies that were to look modest when compared with the further cuts made by the new Conservative government as the recession deepened and money had to be found to finance the soaring social security costs of spiralling unemployment.

Thatcher's government

took office with a self-consciously radical strategy involving a 'rolling back of the state', the dismantling of corporatist forms, and the implementation of liberal free-market policies aiming to reverse economic decline.

(Graham and Prosser 1988: 3)

Central to the economic policy was the monetarist strategy of reducing inflation by letting unemployment rise. Yet the far-reaching, complex, radical-right programme was not merely concerned with monetarist means for putting the economy back on course. It also constituted a total politico-ideological agenda, the primary aim of which was to ensure that no further encroachments on the power of capital were made by labour – either via the unions (they were to be smashed) or via the welfare state (it was to be dismantled). This was an agenda which replaced the ethic of collective social welfare informing consensus politics since the late 1950s, with the classical liberal ethic of individualism and self-reliance (Hall 1983: 29). Because housing, education and welfare benefits were targeted for the most severe cuts at the same time as unemployment was being allowed to rise to unprecedented levels, the brunt of Thatcher's frontal attack on labour was increasingly borne by the young, especially 16 and 17-year-old school-leavers, the majority of whom lost all entitlement to income support under the provisions of the Social Security Act, 1988. The 'new welfare' and the 'new penality', both brutally fashioned to cow and debilitate the 'new, unattached' young, will be fully discussed in Chapter 2. First, though, a look at housing policy under Thatcher. For, of all the other policies designed to gild monetarism with a populist edge, Thatcherite housing policy, combined with high youth unemployment and punitive cuts in young people's welfare eligibility, was central to the production of 1980s and 1990s youth homelessness.

'A property-owning democracy'? No place for the homeless

The complexities of financing housing resulted in both Labour and Conservative governments taking a primarily pragmatic approach to housing provision during the 30 years prior to 1979. Thatcher's New Right housing policy, by contrast, was driven by one primary aim: realization of the 1955 Tory promise of achieving a 'property-owning democracy'. After 1979, promotion of home ownership through sales of council houses, and the continuation of favourable tax rebates on mortgages for all owner-occupiers, accelerated a trend that had been Conservative policy since the 1950s. 'By 1983, 59 per cent of the electorate were homeowners' (Daunton 1987: 81).

What was the situation for non-homeowners? The number of private dwellings available for renting had more than halved between 1961 and 1989 (Greve 1991: 20), and 85 per cent of properties still owned by councils in 1986 required repairs (Audit Commission 1986, cited in Franklin 1988: 3). Moreover, councils which in the early 1980s had persisted in attempting to fulfil electoral promises to house the homeless and improve existing accommodation were threatened under the 1984 Rates Act with a disproportionate loss of central government grant (a penalty known as rate capping) if they set rates above a government-defined limit. Further frustration was experienced at the government's refusal to allow councils to spend more than 25 per cent of the revenue from council houses on projects for housing the homeless.

The ideological thrust behind the determination to reduce public housing provision was towards a property-based individualism guaranteeing freedom to consume (and consume and consume!) independently of the social controls of a bureaucratic and paternalistic state. Writing at the end of the 1980s Peter Malpass (1990: 38) argues that:

> In retrospect it is clear that council housing has never been allowed to develop as a threat to the dominance of market-based provision. On the contrary, it has played a supportive, complementary role, underpinning the private sector. Having originated and grown mainly as housing for the rather better off within the working class, council housing has become subject to gathering pressures to transform it into a residual tenure for the least well off.

Alternatively, Michael Heseltine, Minister of State for the Environment in 1981, offered an explanation for the apparently widespread support for home ownership that completely ignored the extent to which both the supply and quality of alternative tenures had been allowed to run down. Performing the old Tory conjuring trick of translating greed into morality, Heseltine claimed that the desire to own one's home was both moral and British:

> There is in this country a deeply ingrained desire for home ownership. The Government believes that this spirit should be fostered. It reflects the wishes of the people, ensures the widespread of wealth through society, encourages a personal desire to improve and modernise one's home, enables people to accrue wealth for their children and stimulates the attitudes of independence and self-reliance that are the bedrock of a free society.
>
> (quoted in Monk and Kleinman 1990: 122)

The implication is clear. People who do not own their homes, or, worse still, are actually homeless, are not only lacking in self-reliance but their existence is a threat to British society. Once this view of homelessness was ideologically and discursively rolled up together with fears of crime, illegitimacy and masterless men on the loose, the time was ripe for punitive measures against a newly-discovered threat – the underclass. As will be seen in Chapter 2, the so-called underclass poor came to be represented as one of the greatest threats to the stability of the property-owning democracy. Accordingly, some of the most vituperative attacks on 'welfare dependants' have been directed at unemployed youth in general, and unmarried mothers, squatters and New Age travellers in particular. Arguably, it could more reasonably be posited that the greatest threat to social stability in the 1980s was the steep increase in inequality. Key findings of the Joseph Rowntree Inquiry into Income and Wealth (Barclay 1995: 13,14,15,20) included evidence that:

- Incomes rapidly became less equal in the 1980s;
- Internationally, the UK was exceptional in the pace and extent of the increase in inequality in the 1980s;
- Since 1979 the lowest income groups have not benefited from economic growth;
- Since 1977 the proportion of the population with less than half the average income has more than trebled;
- Between 1979 and 1992, the proportion of men aged 18–24 who were working fell from 86 to 73 per cent; for women aged 18–24 the percentage stayed at 65 per cent – in contrast to the rise for older women. For both men and women the relative wages of those under 25 have fallen, particularly for the lowest paid.

Whether or not social inequality is a threat to social stability (some would argue that it is, in essence, a manifestation of social *in*stability), it is certainly another piece for inclusion in the homelessness jigsaw.

Youth homelessness produced

Defining youth homelessness

It will not have escaped the reader's notice that no attempt has yet been made in these pages to define homelessness. This has been deliberate. There *is* no generally agreed definition of homelessness. The narrowest possible definition is, of course, that of literal rooflessness, the total lack of any shelter. But the term 'home' has come to have cultural and ideological meanings going way beyond having a roof over one's head. To add to the confusion, while it has been in the interest of governments to define homelessness as narrowly as possible, it has been in the interest of groups campaigning on behalf of the homeless to be very catholic in their definitions. Helpfully, in 1981 a Department of Environment study suggested a very broad definition of homelessness, an index incorporating the so-called 'hidden homeless' (often only hidden insofar as they are not officially recognized as homeless) as well as the more 'visible' (roofless, or otherwise recognized) homeless (Department of the Environment 1981). Homelessness in their research was defined as involving persons:

- being without shelter now;
- facing the loss of shelter within one month;
- living in a situation of no security of tenure and being forced to seek

alternative accommodation within a time period which the client considers to be immediate; for example, potential dischargees from institutions of all types; people living with friends or relatives in overcrowded conditions; or illegal tenancies;
• living in reception centres, crash pads, derelict buildings, squats, (unlicensed) hostels, cheap lodging-houses, cheap hotels and boarding houses.

Because the struggle over the meanings of homelessness is integral both to the governance of youth homelessness and the more fundamental management of social change, statutory definitions are discussed more fully in Chapter 2, while emergent discourses on homelessness are detailed throughout the book. In one sense, of course, interrogation of the meanings of youth homelessness was one of the main objectives of the Shropshire and Three Cities projects which together provide ethnographic data and illustrative quotations in later chapters. Just now, it must suffice to say that when the term 'youth' is used in this book it generally refers to men and women, single or married, aged 26 and under. None the less, because of the variety of age groupings used in the homelessness research evidence quoted, sometimes the upper age limit for the 'young, single homeless' category in the research data cited includes persons up to the age of 30, and often it is not known whether the figures relate only to persons without partners, or whether they include all persons who are literally unmarried but who may nonetheless have a partner. As far as the term homelessness is concerned, the most useful definitional approaches I have come across are those by Watson and Austerberry (1986) and Jahiel (1987).

Watson and Austerberry suggest an understanding of homelessness based on a house to homelessness continuum, with literal rooflessness (sleeping rough) at one extreme and absolute security of tenure at the other. Temporary accommodation such as hostels, licensed squats, and insecure rentals would come in between and even mortgaged homes could be included. Adoption of such a continuum, they argue, would enable the use of such categories as 'potential homelessness' (pertaining, for example, to all inmates of institutions such as hospitals and hostels who could and would live outside if appropriate permanent accommodation were to be made available, and who would therefore require accommodation if their institutions turned them out). Insofar as Austerberry and Watson are concerned with *degrees* of homelessness, theirs is a quantitative approach. Jahiel's is more qualitative, in that it recognizes that to some extent 'homelessness' is in the eye of the beholder.

The value of Jahiel's conceptualization inheres in its recognition that there are both subjective and objective dimensions to, and differences in, housing need. Appropriately, it distinguishes between: 'benign homelessness' – when a person is temporarily homeless (according to any definition) but actually has the personal, social and material resources to be housed fairly speedily when required; and 'malign homelessness' – when a person is homeless (on any definition) and has either no or insufficient access to the resources necessary to reverse the homelessness situation. This is a qualitative rather than a quantitative distinction and allows, for example, differentiation between people living in the same hostel, but under different circumstances; e.g. one person might be living there out of choice in order to save up to buy a flat, but could in fact afford to move to secure tenure housing if cheaper alternatives ceased to be available; another, on the other hand, might be forced to live in the hostel (without security of tenure and suffering personal hardship because of the hopelessness of his or her housing prospects) solely because the otherwise uncongenial hostel is the only affordable place on offer. On Jahiel's definitions, the former's situation would fit the benign homeless category, while the latter's homelessness would be seen as malign. In the brief summary of research into 1980s and 1990s youth homelessness which follows as much information as possible will be given about *what* was counted as homelessness, and/or *who* was counted as homeless in each investigation.

Statistics on youth homelessness

Reliable calculations of the number of young homeless are extremely difficult to obtain, primarily because of the definitional problems described above. In the early 1990s Shelter estimated that there were 'between two and three thousand people sleeping rough in Central London alone and . . . maybe as many as 5000 people sleeping rough in the rest of the country' (Shelter 1991: 4). Overall, Shelter estimated that there were 156,000 young, homeless people in Britain, including the 50,000 between the ages of 16 and 19 estimated by Centrepoint (provider of hostels for young, single people) to be living in central London (Shelter 1991: 5). By 1994, Shelter was estimating that in 1993 'up to 8600 people slept rough' (Shelter 1994c). According to Killeen (1992: 189):

> The extent of the problem is highlighted by the observations of the Foyer des Jeunes Travailleurs (a French organization which provides hostel places for young people), that Britain has the most acute problem of youth homelessness of all European countries.

Getting figures for specific areas outside London is more difficult than obtaining them for the capital. There are at least some official figures for each of the areas in which the Three Cities and Shropshire Studies took place, as well as some estimates from other independent research conducted in North Staffordshire (Smith and Gilford 1991). The figures from Shropshire are particularly interesting because they indicate that by the beginning of the 1990s there was a significant problem of rural homelessness in England. However, it should always be borne in mind that comparative analysis of local homelessness statistics is repeatedly hampered by the problems of definition involved in their collection and/or presentation.

The Three Cities research was concerned with questions of youth home-lessness in Manchester, Birmingham and Stoke-on-Trent. In Manchester, during the quarter April to June 1994, 501 young, single people under the age of 26 presented themselves as homeless (Manchester City Council 1994). In Birmingham in 1991, of the 2573 single, homeless people who approached the Birmingham City Council for help, 299 (12 per cent) were under the age of 18 (Birmingham City Council 1992). In Smith and Gilford's (1991) study in North Staffordshire, of 2126 young people aged 25 and under contacting all agencies in the area during the 12 months from April 1990, just over half were single, i.e. with no partner and not known to be pregnant, and nearly three-quarters were deemed by the agen-cies to be homeless or potentially homeless. In the Shropshire study, Carlen estimated that the total number of young single homeless people under 26 years of age (unmarried, with or without partners), including the 'hidden' homeless, was 1500 (Carlen and Wardhaugh 1992).

The main characteristics of single homelessness in 1990 as identified by the best research available at the beginning of the decade (Greve 1991) were as follows:

- most single homeless people were young;
- the average age of the homeless was falling;
- homelessness was increasing 50 per cent faster outside London;
- homelessness was growing fastest among young people, especially those in the 16–18 age group;
- women outnumbered men in the 16–18 age group, though previously men were in the majority within homeless groups.

(Randall 1992)

What, then, has caused such large-scale homelessness, and who are the homeless?

The causes of homelessness

There are two types of answer to the question 'What causes homelessness?' – the empiricist and the social structuralist. The former looks at the pre-senting characteristics of currently homeless people and then provides a teleological explanation based on those attributes; e.g. 'homeless people often come from "broken" families ergo the cause of homelessness is family discord'. The circularity of this type of argument should be obvious. Social structuralist explanations describe and analyse any changes in law, economy and political and ideological cultures which, they argue, have resulted in more (or fewer) people becoming homeless.

In recent years the empiricist and social structuralist approaches have tended to become polarized, with the dominant paradigms most fre-quently stressing structural factors, and putting a particular emphasis on the politico-economic management of the housing market. Crudely put, the debate nowadays is between those who insist that homelessness is a question of housing (and that therefore the answer lies in the causes of a shortage of affordable housing, and those who, at the other extreme, still see homelessness as part and parcel of a generalized underclass feckless-ness, eternally threatening to market morality and well-being, but con-tained (and concurrently encouraged) in the 1960s and 1970s by the 'nanny' welfare state.

Yet even social structuralists who eschew explanations giving primacy to individual pathologies recognize that during times of great social inequality a pernicious mix of ideological and structural factors bear down most heavily (or even exclusively in the cases of racism and sexism) on certain social groups. It has already been explained (in the Introduction) that this book's prime concern is with the political production of youth homelessness as a site of struggle over social change and the possibilities of identity. Accordingly, much of its focus is upon the mediation and trans-lation of structural factors into a knowledge of homelessness which is qual-itatively different to any one of its structural *causes*. The discursive strategy in this section is, therefore, limited to setting out a selection of the main social stucturalist discourses on the causes of homelessness. In Chapters 2 and 3 their plausibility and coherence will be repeatedly fractured and called into question by the vocabularies and lexicons of homelessness wherein the homelessness-governing agencies and homeless populations themselves are constituted.

So, the agenda for answering the question posed above about the causes of homelessness is: first, to outline the *structural* causes of homelessness, including both the structural causes for lack of affordable housing *and* the structural reasons for certain groups of people being more likely to become homeless than others; second, to examine the *precipitating* causes of home-lessness, that is, to recognize that the precipitation of homelessness occurs at the collision of biographical difference and structural systemicities; and, third, to look at the demographic characteristics of those most likely to be caught up in such collisions. Finally, this chapter (and to mollify anyone who has started to mutter about 'deterministic explanation') will describe and analyse some contemporary modes of resistance to homelessness con-junctures.

Structural causes of homelessness in general

The gap between incomes and the price of housing

Between 1980 and 1990 house prices more than doubled while earnings failed to increase at the same rate. During the same period there was, as we have already seen, a sharp increase in poverty and a widening inequality of income. 'In April 1990 there were 8.5 million people living below the Low Pay Unit's "decency threshold" of £172.13 per week' (Oldman 1991: 2).

Between 1979 and 1989,

the real annual income of the average household increased . . . by
£2523, whereas the income of the poorest 20 per cent fell . . . by £160
. . . the income of the richest 20 per cent increased on average . . . by
£7986.

(Townsend 1991: 3)

Decrease in the numbers of housing units available for renting

There were three main reasons for the decline in the availability of homes
to rent: first, there was a sharp reduction in council house building, 'from
well over 100,000 houses a year in the mid-seventies to 15,000 in 1990'
(Greve 1991: 18). Second, the 1980 Housing Act introduced the right (for
tenants) to buy council houses and flats at a discount; in the next 10 years
'the social sector of housing [was] depleted by the sale of over 1.5 million
council houses under the "Right to Buy" policy' (Greve 1991: 19). Third,
the number of private dwellings available for renting fell by more than a
half to 1.8 million (less than 8 per cent of the total stock) between 1961
and 1989 (Greve 1991: 20). The situation was aggravated by the poor condition of existing council stock and by the government's refusal to allow
more than 25 per cent of the revenue from council house sales to be spent
on provision for the homeless.

Structural causes of youth homelessness

Affordability gap

The gap between incomes and the price of housing was especially wide
for young people who in the 1980s experienced an increase in school-
leaver unemployment, at the same time as the real incomes of the lowest
paid young workers actually fell. Punitive changes in welfare support were
therefore directed at unemployed school-leavers who might be tempted
to think that being on social security was better than being in a low-paid
dead-end job. Changes in social security authorized by the Social Security
Act, 1986 were implemented in April 1988. The major changes affecting
the young homeless were that 'urgent needs payments', allowing a person
with no money to book into cheap accommodation, were abolished and
replaced with repayable 'crisis loans', and one-off and non-repayable
grants for clothes, bedding and other necessities were abolished and
replaced with repayable loans at official discretion (see Gosling 1988 for
some examples of how this discretion was used). Furthermore, under the
Social Security Act, 1988 most 16 and 17-year-olds 'lost all entitlement to
income support' (NCH 1991: 14). Killeen (1992: 193) has detailed how,
under the 'new pattern of youth welfare', young people have been discriminated against not only in relation to income support and urgent
needs payments, but also in relation to housing benefit and the new community charge. This new era of repressive disciplinary welfare (as distinct

from the previous era of facilitative disciplinary welfare) is discussed more fully in Chapter 2.

Decrease in availability of rented accommodation

The effect on young people of the housing shortage was not properly appreciated in the early 1980s because of a generalized ideological refusal to acknowledge that many young people living at home, in institutions, or with friends or relatives actually wanted a home of their own (NCH Fact-file 1992: 35). This refusal to recognize the changing housing needs of young people has helped to perpetuate youth homelessness.

Inappropriateness of available accommodation to changing family structures and/or lifestyles

The lack of fit between young people's housing requirements and the limited range of housing on offer is indicative of the many changes that have occurred in household arrangements and lifestyles in the last quarter of the century, and which have frequently provoked innovations in house design. Unfortunately, they have seldom resulted in new types of tenure. Given the central place that housing was accorded in Thatcher's vote-winning and pleb-pacification programmes, it is not surprising that since 1979 there has been a politically motivated attack on many new types of household, especially those headed by single mothers or homosexuals. Nor, in that context, is it surprising that much of the agency management of youth poverty and youth homelessness is also a site of struggle over contested lifestyles (see Chapter 2).

Poverty and inequality

Between 1980 and 1990 over a million households – containing 1.5 million children – were accepted by local authorities as homeless (Greve 1991: 13). In 1993 alone, unemployment, poverty and high interest rates resulted in 58,540 homes being repossessed by mortgage lenders (Shelter 1994b). When homes are repossessed and families go into bed and breakfast accommodation teenage members often refuse to accompany them into what they see as being the modern-day workhouse. Instead, they attempt to live with friends in private homes. When these arrangements break down the youngsters are frequently precipitated into the revolving-door syndrome of hostel, sleeping roofless, various other makeshift arrangements, hostel – and so on.

Youth unemployment and poverty adversely affect family relationships even when the parents themselves have no housing problems. A significant number of teenage children leave home after family rows occasioned by their lack of employment and subsequent inability either to contribute to household expenses or to finance their own leisure needs (see Hutson and Jenkins 1987: 46; Wallace 1987: 46).

Structural causes of youth homelessness: by specific groups of people for whom there is underprovision

In addition to the structural conditions causing homelessness and confronting all people at the moment when insecurity of tenure (in the case of a tenant) or impossibility of continued residence (e.g. in the case of an incest victim) occasions a move from existing accommodation, there are other structural conditions to which specific groups of young people are especially vulnerable.

Women

Women have, historically, been underprovided for as tenants and home-owners in their own right (Austerberry and Watson 1983; Watson and Austerberry 1986), a policy tradition embedded in the long-dominant ideology that the nuclear family should be heterosexual and headed by a male breadwinner. Moreover, even though there are indications that in the 16–19 age group more young women than men are running away from home, studies of homelessness again and again reveal that there are very few all-women hostels. Hendessi (1992) has claimed that many young women become homeless as a result of sexual and/or physical abuse. Of those women who do leave home because they can no longer put up with the abuse, a considerable number are too afraid of men to seek a place in mixed accommodation (Carlen 1990). In 1977, a consultative document on housing policy recognized that 'battered women' had especially urgent housing needs (Department of the Environment 1977), but later surveys have continued to stress that women's homelessness is more likely to be hidden than men's (O'Mahoney 1988). There is also some evidence that homeless women are likely to be seen to be violating gender stereotypes of femininity by their apparent failure to get a bed for the night (Carlen 1983a; Carlen and Christina 1985). Certainly, one consequence of women's particularly low incomes (Pascall 1986; Townsend et al. 1987; Millar 1993) is that they are more likely than men to be affected by housing's 'affordability gap' (Ginsburg and Watson 1992: 151). About a fifth of all homelessness is precipitated by the breakdown of a relationship with a partner, and therefore separated or divorced women are especially disadvantaged. Prime Minister Thatcher, along with many others then and now, espoused and propagated the idea that young unmarried women deliberately get pregnant in order to jump the housing queue (Ginsburg and Watson 1992: 154). Consequently, and as will be seen in Chapter 2, their situation under the homelessness legislation is under constant threat (for a sensitive account of the lives of some homeless women in the United States, see Liebow 1993).

Young persons leaving local authority care

Every year, 8500 young people 16–18 leave care in England and Wales
– many of them to become homeless.

(Greve 1991: 16)

At the beginning of the 1990s, a report by Centrepoint (1990) suggested
that 40 per cent of young homeless people have been in care. Lack of prep-
aration for non-institutional living, homelessness and poverty have been
listed as the all-embracing problems confronting young people leaving
local authority residential care between the ages of 16 and 19 (e.g. Stein
and Maynard 1985). In 1984 an official report emphasized the need for
'continuing care' (House of Commons 1984) and under the 1989 Children
Act local authorities were given new powers and had new duties imposed
upon them 'to provide (in certain circumstances) accommodation for
young people up to the age of 21, whether or not they have previously
been in the care of the local authority' (Greve 1991: 37). Additionally, they
were given a general duty to 'befriend' and 'advise' any child leaving care
until that child reached the age of 21 (Department of Health 1989). As late
as 1993, however, a national survey of local authority provision found that
a majority of social service departments were failing to fulfil their responsibilities to homeless 16 and 17-year-olds under the 1989 Children Act
(McClusky 1993: 2). In the Three Cities Research, 42 of the 100 young
people contacted had been in care for some period prior to interview.

Ex-prisoners

Imprisonment is a partial cause of homelessness because: it leads to family
breakup; it reduces family income; single people often lose tenancies while
in prison; and ex-prisoners are not seen as desirable tenants. Ex-prisoners
are prominent among those who are repeatedly caught in the revolving-
door syndrome of prison, hospital, supported accommodation, rooflessness, and so on. This is not only because homeless offenders have a much
higher reconviction rate than not-homeless offenders, but also because
their homelessness is often a salient factor in the courts' decision either to
remand them in custody (Casale 1989: 35) or sentence them to imprisonment (Carlen 1983a). In 1991 the Prison Reform Trust reported that in
answer to questions posed by a national prison survey carried out on behalf
of the Prison Service 'some 12 per cent of convicted prisoners said that they
had no permanent accommodation at the time they were imprisoned'
(Prison Reform Trust 1991).

Black and ethnic minority people

There is considerable evidence that black people and people from non-
black ethnic minority groups suffer from direct racial discrimination in the
housing market (Smith 1989; Ginsburg and Watson 1992). They are also

indirectly disadvantaged because of the difficulties they experience in the job market (Greve 1991). Yapp (1987) found that amongst the residents of London night shelters discriminatory and racist behaviour and language were often directed at black people. In June 1992, the Commission for Racial Equality reported that 'homelessness and its disproportionate impact on ethnic minorities continued to be a concern' during 1991.

Rural youth

The 'affordability gap' takes a specific form in rural areas where the prices of houses are pushed up by wealthy commuters and town-dwellers in search of second homes. The low average wages of local inhabitants (in 1992 in south Shropshire, for instance, they were 20 per cent below the national average) ensures that they are not able to compete in the housing market (see Bramley 1990). The report of the Archbishops' Commission on Rural Areas (1990: 95) recalled that 'concerns about the rising cost of housing, particularly in relation to levels of rural income, have been voiced since at least the mid-1970s'. Yet concern seems to have been slow to gather momentum. This may have been because, as Lewis and Talbot (1987: 129) argue, homelessness in the countryside is more likely to be hidden by the greater use of so-called mobile homes and holiday lettings, as well as by the perhaps greater incidence of two generations sharing one home. That notwithstanding, in 1992 Lambert *et al.* reported that in the preceding four years rural homelessness had increased at a faster rate than urban home-lessness. Additional reasons for the increase may have included: the extra low supply of council houses in rural areas where the 'right to buy' policy has had particularly serious effects (see Clark 1991); the decrease in the amount of accommodation tied to jobs in agriculture; and restrictive plan-ning policies resulting in a lack of economies of scale in new house-build-ing, one consequence being that new housing in villages has been predominantly at the most expensive end of the market (see Robinson 1990; Shucksmith 1990). In short, the lives of poor people in rural England at the end of the twentieth century are no more idyllic than they were for the rural poor of earlier centuries (see Button 1990; Carlen and Wardhaugh 1991).

People of homosexual orientation

Discrimination against people of homosexual orientation was evident in the well-publicized anti-homosexuality clause 5.28 of the Local Govern-ment Act, 1988. Green *et al.* (1988) expressed fears about its impact on housing and homelessness when they commented:

> Many lesbians become homeless or experience housing difficulties as a direct result of other people's hostile reaction to their sexuality. They have suffered hostility and even physical violence in temporary and

shared accommodation and further discrimination and prejudice in trying to find suitable permanent housing.

Some councils and organizations have begun to acknowledge and respond to the housing needs of lesbians and gay men in the face of hostility, prejudice and physical attack. They may now withdraw their services for fear of prosecution under the Local Government Act 1988 which prohibits the 'intentional promotion of homosexuality' while giving little guidance as to how this will be interpreted.

This is but one example of how homelessness may be produced as a by-product of battles about citizenship and alternative lifestyles. Oldman (1990: 6) reported that 'in 1987 six out of ten calls to lesbian and gay switchboards concerned homelessness', while 'the London Gay Teenage Group found 11% of young people had been made homeless because of their sexuality'.

People with disabilities

People with disabilities which are part-cause of their low incomes are particularly vulnerable to homelessness at times when the affordability gap between incomes and the price of housing is wide. The group seen to be most vulnerable is comprised of people with a miscellany of unusual behavioural repertoires, especially those clinically defined as having 'personality disorders' (Carlen 1983a, 1990). Others become homeless merely because sharp competition for decent accommodation during times of severe housing shortage makes it impossible for them to retain tenancies if they are subject to prolonged periods of either hospitalization or debilitation (e.g. from incapacitating conditions such as alcoholism and/or other drug addiction, epilepsy, chronic illness or social isolation).

Precipitating causes of homelessness

The structural causes of homelessness described above exist independently of any individual's awareness of them; indeed, they frequently remain obscure to people even after they have become homeless. The precipitating causes, on the other hand, are those immediate and situational ones which young people readily recall when they are asked to account for their homeless situation, for instance a family row or discharge from an institution. The Central Office of Information estimated that in 1991, the main reasons put forward for their homelessness by applicants for local authority housing were:

that family and friends were no longer prepared to accommodate them (42%); the breakdown of a marriage or other relationship with a partner (16%); the loss of a private rented dwelling (27%); [and] mortgage arrears (12%).

(Central Office of Information 1993)

It should be noted here, however (and it will be expounded upon at greater length in Chapter 2), that available evidence suggests that, for a variety of reasons, the vast majority of homeless people under the age of 26 do not attempt to get accepted on to their local authorities' housing (waiting) lists.

> In 1993 local authorities accepted 2017 young single people in non-priority need in England. This figure represents less than 1.5% of the total number of households accepted as homeless in 1993.
>
> (Department of the Environment, 1993)

Resisting home, 'homes' and homelessness

Campaigning and official concerns about homelessness are most frequently related to the quality and degree of shelter, safety, tenure and amenity of people's accommodation. A less explicit official housing agenda part-controls the regulation of youth and the management of social and cultural change. So let us take a preliminary look at some of the slightly different referents associated with the concepts of 'home', 'homes' and 'homelessness'. It is often as a result of calling into question or resisting these more qualitative and normative connotations that 'runaways', New Age travellers and a variety of other 'homeless' persons find themselves both without a 'home' in the more conventional and material sense, and stigmatized for being 'homeless' in the more ideological and moral sense. In other words, while the meanings of both 'home' and 'homelessness' are multifaceted, the strategic meanings of 'home' to 'homeless' persons may be completely asymmetrical to those constructed by housing bureaucracy officials to define and assess 'homelessness' claims to public housing. This is especially so when people are unable or unwilling to buy into the conventional, official, consumerist or ideological meanings of home, 'homes' and homelessness.

Home, 'homes' and homelessness . . . when words fail

First (but not always) there is *home as shelter* in the material sense. Then there is *home as consumption,* the site of domesticity which is either owned or for which rent is paid, and wherein may be collected all kinds of material goods with both economic and symbolic value. Third, there is *home as emotional retreat* – as in the sentimental song 'No place like home', and in the dictionary definition, 'a place . . . where one properly belongs, in which one's affections centre, or where one finds rest, refuge or satisfaction' (Onions 1983: 976) (see Snow and Anderson 1993: 7–8; Jencks 1994: 3 for similar discussions). Fourth, and ironically, there are *'homes'* – as in children's homes – the statutory (and often compulsory) shelters provided by the state for those towards whom it has a duty of care.

Next there is 'homelessness': literally, *the lack of home* on any of the foregoing definitions and taxonomies; plus, '*homelessness as legitimated housing need*' as construed by any of the 'homelessness' adjudicators and according to a mix of moral, economic, legal, ideological and political interests. And lastly, and eccentrically, 'homelessness' as the catch-all metaphor for a variety of poverty-stricken or otherwise socially question-able conditions. Surfacing in the allegory of 'homelessness as an index of social breakdown', this latter-day trope is most frequently embedded in discourses framing a myriad of media and campaigning interests. Although some of these interests are benign, 'homelessness as social breakdown' also plays on traditional and popular fears that shadowy threats to self and society are embodied in the indigent itinerant. Which is, of course, why this latter understanding of homelessness is so vehemently opposed as a scurrilous slur by many who (on more literal definitional criteria) appear to be prime candidates for homelessness status.

And the Other of homelessness discourses? Maybe those who reject conventional ideologies of 'home' and 'homelessness', and fight to carve out from fragments of those discourses new, or presently non-legitimated (or barely tolerated) ways of living; or maybe the struggle to think the unthinkable about homelessness – and why the sight of the homeless on the streets can stir up such ambivalent feelings of pain, threat, guilt, blame, irritation, and agnosticism (see the discussion at the end of Chapter 2).

There have always been originals whose alternative lifestyles have been feared as threats to property and capitalist 'order'. Consider now three present-day groupings of unconventionals whose modes of living bring them into conflict with family, welfare authorities, homeowners, home-lessness agencies, or the law.

Runaways

In England the term runaway is reserved for young persons under the age of 17 who have left home or substitute care illegally. In 1992 it was esti-mated that 43,000 young people run away from home or substitute care each year, and that between them they account for 102,000 running away incidents (Abrahams and Mungall 1992). There is some evidence to suggest that young women are more likely to run away from home than young men (Rees 1993: 4).

The link between running away and youth homelessness is a tenuous one. Many runaways are what have been termed 'crisis homeless' – they stay away for a very short time after some kind of upset before returning home, and many of them will never be known as runaways at all (Stock-ley *et al.* 1991). Others, by contrast, run away repeatedly, making new con-tacts and becoming ever-more (or ever-less) streetwise, until, on their seventeenth birthday, they cease to be runaways and (not having anywhere new to call 'home') come of age as 'young homeless' (see Simons and Whit-beck 1991, referred to in Stein *et al.* 1994).

Why do young people run away from home or substitute care in the first place? And why, in a minority of cases, do they repeatedly abscond until eventually they seldom (or never) go home?

There is no evidence to support the myth that runaways take off in search of the bright lights. Rather, latest research in England is agreed that although the immediate (precipitating) causes of young people running away are extremely varied, the causes most frequently cited by runaways and the people who work with them is related to family conflict – often involving physical, mental, emotional or sexual abuse (see Rees 1993 and Stein *et al.* 1994). When they run away again and again it is most likely to be because no one investigated, listened to, or took seriously their reasons for going off on the previous occasions; in sum, the problem occasioning the first absconding had either not been addressed by any responsible adult upon their return home (or to substitute care), or it had been dealt with in such a way that the original situation was aggravated (Newman 1989; Rees 1993: 5). Taking runaways into the care of the local authority does not appear to put an end to their running.

Available evidence suggests that rates of absconding from residential care are much higher than rates of absconding from families (Rees 1993). However, it should also be borne in mind that, first, many runaways from care have previously absconded from the family home; second, absconding from residential care is much more likely to be officially reported and thereafter seen as such than are very short, albeit unauthorized, absences from the family home; and third, Rees (1993: 42–3) found that though only two of the 28 (7 per cent) 'residential care' runaways whom she surveyed claimed to have been unhappy most of the time in their current placement, as many as 10 out of 25 (40 per cent) said they had been so when they had last lived with their families, with the comparable figure for those who had lived with foster parents being six out of 14 (43 per cent).

These caveats notwithstanding, there *is* serious cause for concern about what goes on in children's homes, not least about the prevalence of institutional abuse in residential homes of all kinds. In particular, a number of official inquiries and news reports have focused attention on the many cases of mental, physical and sexual abuse perpetrated on young persons in the residential care of the local authorities (e.g. Levy and Kahan 1990; and see *The Independent*, 15 June 1994: 3 and 19 July 1994: 2 for reports of the jailing of a former deputy head of a children's home for the sexual abuse of teenage boys in his care). Recognition of the obvious fact that young persons in residential care are there because of some pre-existing problem or family misfortune need not close our eyes to evidence that so-called 'care' regimes can exacerbate existing problems and even create new ones (see Carlen 1987, 1988, 1992; Carlen *et al.* 1992). Runaways from care being precipitated into homelessness is a prefatory example of the homelessness syndrome which in the next chapter will be analysed as 'agency-maintained homelessness'. The professionals interviewed in the research of Stein *et al.* (1994: 52) also emphasized the impact of social structural 'economic factors on both the family (in terms of poverty), and the residential system (in terms of shortage of resources)'.

What seems certain from the information culled from all reliable sources (and most especially from young people who have run away themselves) is that the vast majority of youngsters who repeatedly run away from family and/or children's homes, and eventually stay away on a permanent or semi-permanent basis, are resisting a way of life that has become intolerable to them. In violating the legal requirement that children under the age of 17 should reside under parental or substitute parental control, absconders also call into question two dominant and conservative ideologies: that home is a haven – regardless of the economic pressures on the household; and that children's homes can provide remedial care – regardless of the financial restrictions on social services budgets, and however meagre the young person's future life chances are in terms of employment, housing and other citizen goods.

Finally, there are the runaway 'novice homeless' who not only resist home and homes, but who also resent the stigma implicit in the 'agency-maintained homelessness' that again and again locks into the allegory of homelessness as social dislocation, and which also, by implication, depicts all houseless or roofless people as having some more pressing personal problem than that of lack of home. These are the young people (more likely to be found among 'care' runaways) who reject the notion that they are not old enough to make their own way in the world independently of adult control and tutelage. Resisting any temptation to run the risk of being returned home or to substitute care as a result of approaching official agencies for shelter or support, they prefer to build up support networks amongst themselves (see O'Mahoney 1988; Stein et al. 1994: 41). These are also the youngsters who, in replying to the question, 'Do you consider yourself homeless?' tend to dismiss it by saying, 'Oh no. I've always had a roof over my head, and I've never begged, or taken drugs, or anything like that'. Other 'novice homeless', however, have developed licit and/or illicit survival strategies involving prostitution, begging or crime. Many of them, in talking of their dubious survival strategies, will contradictorily both deny and invoke the allegory of 'homelessness as threat', either by claiming that government legislation or policies have literally left them with no access to alternative lifestyles and/or that as outcasts of society they need owe no allegiance to its laws (see Chapters 2, 3 and 4 for development of these themes and the ethnographic material used to illustrate them).

New Age travellers

Almost as much controversy centres on the term New Age traveller as it does on the group of people usually denoted by it. Indeed, many readers will protest that the term is nothing more than a convenient shorthand invented by the media for the folk-devilling of a variety of picturesque nomads. I agree. The term is being used here merely to distinguish a group of travellers with newer traditions and shorter histories than the more traditional Romany gypsies or Irish travellers.

Not much serious research has been conducted into the situation of the increasing numbers of young homeless people 'moving from sleeping rough into vehicles and caravans, thus becoming travellers' (Davis *et al.* 1994: 1). In 1992/3, therefore, researchers for the Children's Society interviewed 98 travellers, nearly all under the age of 30 (Davis *et al.* 1994). Part of their investigation set out to discover why people become travellers. The researchers concluded that

> the decision to become travellers was determined far more by 'push factors' – the need to get away from a set of circumstances which were dangerous and intolerable – than by 'pull factors', which would involve a positive choice of a travelling lifestyle.
>
> (Davis *et al.* 1994: 7)

None the less, they also found that 'one third of the travellers involved in the study . . . had made a conscious and deliberate choice to become a traveller' and, moreover, that '*all* . . . considered the way of life to be positive and constructive' (Davis *et al.* 1994: 7, 3; italics in original).

> The way of life offers a sense of community and identity. It also presents an opportunity for cheap living. It was particularly attractive to those . . . who had felt socially isolated or rejected. For example, *without exception*, travellers in the study who had previously been in bed and breakfast accommodation or unsatisfactory housing considered the travelling lifestyle to be far preferable. This was particularly true of traveller women with children.
>
> (Davis *et al.* 1994: 4; italics in original)

Thus although 'only two of the 98 travellers . . . argued that they had an existing alternative to travelling', and although 'the study consistently found links between poverty, homelessness and the decision to travel or to continue to travel' (Davis *et al.* 1994: 7, 5), it still seems that for many of them the entry into travelling had been the endpoint of a series of resistances to increasingly impossible living conditions, an endpoint that had resulted in some of them, at least, achieving a self-enhancing sense of independence born of community interdependence.

> For young, single, homeless people travelling is a chance to obtain viable accommodation without a great deal of capital, given that they receive so little assistance in obtaining housing. Furthermore, the acceptance of, and care for, those new to travelling was evident on many sites . . . The level of care, particularly for young homeless people and other vulnerable people, led one etablished new age traveller to describe some sites as constituting an 'alternative social services' . . . Particularly for young people in the study, living successfully as a traveller imparted a sense of self-worth and of control over their lives.
>
> (Davis *et al.* 1994: 4)

Hostile to hostel rough sleepers

A number of young people sleep rough because they will not accept the only alternative – a place in a night shelter or hostel. The reasons are three-fold.

First of all, hostel rents are considered to be inordinately high, taking up too great a proportion of the wages of residents doing paid work, and leaving those on benefits with ridiculously little money for food or other requirements. The Department of Environment survey (Anderson *et al.* 1993: ix) of 2000 homeless people undertaken in 1991 found that

> The average total income received in the previous week was low com-pared with the general population of households: £39 among people in hostels and B&Bs, £39 among those in day centres and £37 among those at soup runs. One in five people who were sleeping rough said they had received no income in the previous week.

Second, some young people, particularly those who have already been in any kind of institutional accommodation, are very resistant to being subject to further rules and regulations, and/or to what is experienced as the general hassle of hostel life. Young people particularly fear being bullied, or falling victim to the sexual attacks or other crimes of which they have heard, witnessed or experienced as being not infrequent features of hostel life.

Finally, a small minority of rough sleepers resist becoming objects of charity and therapy by refusing to claim any benefits whatsoever. This means that they cannot pay for any board and lodgings at all. In their case, resistance is not so much to hostel life but to the loss of self-esteem they will suffer if they become suppliants for what they see as charity. These are the transient or intermittent rough sleepers who also resist having their lives brought under the moral surveillance of social workers in hostels where their 'other' problems will be addressed. And these are the ones, too, who are most likely to say that they would rather sleep in a cardboard box than lose their self-respect.

Endpiece

The economic and ideological landscapes of itinerancy, homelessness, poverty, and inequality have been sketched in, the political battlelines have been drawn. Chapter 2 examines the ways in which the Thatcherite state of the 80s and early 90s attempted to govern its outcast youth. With the decline of welfare in the 1980s, criminal justice itself was increasingly seen to be punishingly expensive, and, accordingly, governments and penologists turned their punitive stare upon community and home as poss-ible, new (and less expensive) sites for the delivery of state punishment. The marginalized, homeless and poverty-stricken young people described in Chapter 1 were brought centre-stage by the homelessness techno-bureaucracies and the 'law'n'order' merchants. While the custodial authorities began to look towards the home and the community as possibly cheaper bearers of the carceral burden, the agencies set up to address homelessness directed their gaze upon the homeless. And they processed them out to such effect that gradually the young homeless were both addressed and accommodated as the 'street people' of the late twentieth century. Accommodated thus, filed, and literally papered over, the power of the 'new homelessness' to shock was gradually lessened.

2 |

THE GOVERNANCE OF
YOUTH HOMELESSNESS

The governance of youth homelessness begins and ends with its definitions. Periodically weighed (and perennially found wanting) on the shift-
ing scales of charity, social justice, criminal justice, political interest and
legal and techno-bureaucratic normalcy, the meanings of youth homelessness have primarily been activated within (and outwith) three of the
state's principal modes of governance: *discipline* (of youth); *legal and techno-
bureaucratic control* (of the homelessness state); and *ideological accommodation* (of threats both to state legitimacy and the ontological well-being
of individuals). The protocols for the governance of youth homelessness
that have surfaced at different times and in different places can be characterized as being (often simultaneously): premodern, insofar as they draw
on primitive fears of disease, contamination and the mysterious and
ambiguous powers of 'otherness'; modernist, insofar as they seek damage
limitation via regimes of deterrence, denial and discipline; and postmodernist, insofar as they can both empower and/or disempower according to the prevailing political conditions within which youth regimes are
fashioned.

In portraying the governance of youth homelessness it is desirable to
pursue a dual track. Though their separate grooves criss-cross and are often
indistinguishable, the two trajectories can be conceptualized as compris-
ing a selection of the discourses and strategies implicated in the governance of homelessness on the one hand, and the governance of youth on
the other.

First this chapter examines the governance of youth, piece-working its
history since 1945. Then the same technique is tried with the governance
of homelessness. The third reshuffle describes how pieces from both trajectories fall into place (or not), contextually squeezed in and out of all
recognition in the contemporary agency-maintenance of youth homelessness. The chapter's closing section argues that any threats to the legitimacy of the British state which might have been posed by the 200,000
young people experiencing acute homelessness each year (Killeen 1992:
189) have been ideologically accommodated. The most effectively accommodative narrative recasts the young unemployed and homeless as being

the socially expendable, but presently threatening, products of a corrosive 'dependency culture' spawned by an always and already inept welfarism.

The governance of youth

In his incisive analysis of the functions of the welfare state, Ian Gough has argued that the welfare state

> simultaneously embodies tendencies to enhance social welfare, to develop the powers of individuals, to exert social control over the blind play of market forces; and tendencies to repress and control people, to adapt them to the requirements of the capitalist economy.
>
> (Gough 1979: 12)

If this thesis is accepted, then, at first sight at least, it goes some way towards explaining why the political management of the welfare state has realized a two-dimensional (and oppositional) disciplinary process, of facilitation and empowerment through pedagogic rule at times of full employment, and of subordination to a repressive (market) rule during times of recession. Yet the disciplinary process itself is an idealization of just one element in governmentality, the other key constituents being *legitimacy* (of the disciplinary rule) and *power* (to enforce it). Cross-cutting the disciplinary apparatus and its effects are all the lines of resistance, delegitimization and state impotency that in undermining old disciplines simultaneously give birth to the new.

Welfare discipline 1945–79

Youth management is about the management of social reproduction and state probity. It has traditionally been assumed that a prime function of government is to ease and assimilate young people into the labour and housing markets with as little disruption as possible. Immediately after World War II, education, training and family welfare policies were seen as the normal mechanisms of smooth transition from adolescence to adulthood. Ideologically, the focus was on the family. Via a pedagogy steeped in the 'psy' disciplines (see Donzelot 1979) social workers and welfare bureaucracies aimed to infuse working-class families with a scientific management of parenting that would also promote a requisite social discipline and harmony.

> This therapeutic familialism was one element in a web of programmes and arguments that enmeshed conjugal, domestic and parental arrangements in the post-war period. The objectives of these programmes were varied, but each entailed the re-valorization of the child-centred family as a site for the emotional investment and self-realization of citizens.
>
> (Rose 1989: 157)

The hard machine of courts, 'approved schools' and Borstal training still existed for the correction of the delinquent children of 'problem families'. With full employment, however, it was generally assumed that young people would settle down fairly quickly, especially when marriage and family came along. Welfare benefits were available for 16 and 17-year-olds who had not found a job, but for those in work the postwar boom in the economy meant that they had more in their pockets to spend than ever before. A general increase in affluence provoked the rise of the new leisure industry with its focus on youth, and this in turn created conditions in which young people could satisfy many of their leisure needs independently of adults. Unfortunately, youth's new affluence was shortlived. By the early 1970s the spending spree was coming to an end, and 'between 1972 and 1977 unemployment among young people in Great Britain rose by 120 per cent compared with a rise of 45 per cent among the working population as a whole' (Manpower Services Commission 1978; quoted in Banks 1992). As well as looking to the global economy for explanations of Britain's diffi-culties, British politicians looked for causes nearer home, and found them . . . in the power of the trade unions and the costs of welfare. The time had come for a more repressive youth and labour discipline.

Repressive discipline 1945–90s

The attack by the New Right on welfare was provoked partly by the ensuing costs of its own deliberate deflationary policies which proved to be so expensive in terms of unemployment benefits. Partly it was the concomi-tant of an ideology of free market individualism that transformed its trans-parently greedy abhorrence of interference with market mechanisms into a morality propounding the virtues of independence, familiness and econ-omic self-sufficiency.

Ironically, given their penchant for repeatedly sneering at the welfare state for inducing a 'culture of dependency', the Thatcher government's attacks on young people's welfare benefits were consistently directed at making them *more* dependent – on parents who were themselves often unemployed and already struggling to make ends meet.

> The cutting, in 1983, of a weekly £3.10 Housing Addition from the benefits of unemployed young people living with their parents was the most clear early step in this direction.
>
> (Killeen 1992: 196)

An excellent summary of the main legislation relating to young people's housing and income is given by Killeen (1992) who explicates three main features of the New Welfarism. First,

> [B]eginning in 1985, the Government has . . . been consistent in seeking to limit financial support for young people living away from their parents' homes. The Board and Lodgings Regulations . . .

introduced limits on the length of time for which unemployed young people under the age of 25 could receive financial assistance to stay in bed and breakfast hotels. Additional criteria were introduced for young people wishing to qualify for this support in addition to the basic requirements for qualification for Income Support.

A joint monitoring exercise by Shelter and the Scottish Council for Single Homeless People in one month in 1985 found fifty-seven people who had become homeless as a consequence of the introduction of the new rules.

(Killeen 1992: 196–7)

The distinctly punitive nature of this measure was underlined by media reports gloating that young unemployed people would no longer be able to draw benefits while living away from home in seaside 'holiday' resorts!

Second, major changes in welfare support for young people were implemented in 1988. Under the new arrangements:

While the level of benefit payments to people aged 25 and over continued in line with the general uprating of benefits, lower rates of Income Support constituted a clear case of discrimination against young people.

(Killeen 1992: 193)

Third, and in addition to changes in Income Support,

The Social Fund ... was introduced as a replacement of Single and Exceptional Needs payments ... which ... were of assistance to young people setting up separate households, in the form of deposits to secure accommodation and grants for basic furniture requirements. For the majority of young applicants, this assistance is no longer available.

(Killeen 1992: 193)

Having explained how Housing Benefit and the Community Charge (which replaced the old rates system) also discriminate against young people, Killeen concluded that:

the most significant action of the Government with respect to young people, has been the withdrawal of the right to Income Support for unemployed young people aged 16 and 17.

(Killeen 1992: 196)

The government's argument is that all unemployed school-leavers should be on a Youth Training Scheme. *Vox populi* declares (as always) that adolescents who are not fully occupied will commit every kind of imaginable mayhem (see examples from Victorian times in Pearson 1975; and from the early 1980s in Mungham 1982). The overall outcome of welfare, housing, educational, training and unemployment policies during the

1980s resulted in a much strengthened disciplining of pauperized and redundant youth *independently of the criminal justice and/or penal systems.*

Even before the international oil crisis of the 1970s had triggered cuts in public expenditure in Britain, the state education system had become the butt of a mass of ill-informed criticism. It was therefore to be expected that the Tories (aided and abetted by the right-wing press) would blame both schools and young people themselves for rising levels of youth unemployment. The schools were to blame because they did not teach their pupils the skills required by industry; young people were to blame because they had priced themselves out of the market (Lee *et al.* 1990: 3; Brown 1991: 90). Two remedial programmes were implemented. Schools (and teachers) were to be brought into line by the Education Act 1988 and its imposition of a national curriculum on all state schools; the Youth Training Scheme (YTS) was to ensure that young people were forced to work at wages employers were prepared to pay. The reported comments of a senior official at the Department of Education and Science in the early 1980s might very well reflect the way in which the Tory establishment responsible for the Education Act 1988 perceived the links between education and the regulation of social mobility and social unrest:

> We are in a period of considerable social change. There may be social unrest, but we can cope with the Toxteths. But if we have a highly educated and idle population we may possibly anticipate more serious social conflict. People must be educated once more to know their place.
>
> (DES official, quoted in Ranson 1984: 241)

Accordingly, the emphasis was now on training, rather than job creation. And when training failed, free market forces could be relied upon to ensure that the children of the poor did not get above their market value. Lee *et al.* (1990: 1) pinpoint the centrality of YTS to the New Right's programme for the governance of youth unemployment when they comment:

> In 1983, through the Youth Training Scheme (YTS), young people became the target of Mrs Thatcher's free-market revolution and its moral programme . . . Trainees' allowances are set low to match their trainee status and to keep down public spending.

Amongst young people (and their parents) the scheme soon fell into disrepute. Too often the training proves to be no training at all, and trainees leave with no more skills than they had when they started. In some areas the bulk of the placements provide skills of which there is already a surplus in the job market; in other areas trainees are paid lower wages to do jobs previously done by adults at a higher rate (Lee *et al.* 1990: 186). YTS, moreover, has widened the historical gap between the trained and the educated (Lee *et al.* 1990: 189). Children from better-off homes tend not to opt for YTS. Instead, they stay on at school and proceed to higher education while their poorer schoolmates do two-year YTS placements before being slung back into the ranks of the 'unskilled' unemployed. Not surprisingly, some youngsters (and their families) resist a 'training' which they sense to be both exploitative and repressive:

I don't think I could stick that YTS thing. (Kathleen)

I work as a labourer. It's better than YTS. (Geoffrey)

We have YTS down where I work. Believe me, they work for their money. (Anita's mother)

YTS is cheap labour at the end of the day, so I think he's better joining the army. (Lenny's mother)

(Carlen et al. 1992: 148–9; cf. Banks 1992: 54;
Allard et al. 1994: 8–9)

Since 1988, unemployed school-leavers 'unreasonably' refusing a YTS place have not been able to claim benefits and for them one has to assume the only legitimate alternative is to live off odd-jobbing, family and friends. If these legitimate sources of sustenance are unavailable, young unemployed people have to explore other ways and means. It is when they are outwith the protection of employment, family and welfare that they are most likely to adopt one of the transient lifestyles which may well bring them into conflict with the law.

Youth and criminal justice 1945–95

During the years 1945 to the early 1970s official explanations of juvenile delinquency see-sawed between structural analyses giving primacy to the still observable material conditions of poverty and lack of opportunity for deprived youngsters, and social psychological explanations which harped on the supposed failure of consumption-oriented families to instil proper moral values in their offspring. As the childcare and juvenile justice systems converged, they stealthily enlarged the sphere of the penal gaze until the Children and Young Persons Act 1969 (CYPA) collapsed the previously operative distinction between the deprived child and the depraved child into one overall duty of state care towards all children and young persons. In future, all children coming to the attention of the authorities would be open to assessment and categorization, as well as possible removal from home, on a variety of penal and non-penal welfare grounds. This rehabilitationist penology reached its zenith in the 1969 Act, and it was the body of criticism directed at the working of the CYPA 1969 which prepared the ground for the rise of the so-called 'justice' model.

After 1969, rehabilitationism was under attack from almost every part of the political spectrum. Leftist critics complained that individualized sentencing discriminated against working-class youths, black people, and gender-deviant young women. Right-wing pundits believed that the so-called alternatives to custody were too lenient and insufficiently deterrent. Lawyers were concerned that the lack of consistency in (individualized) sentencing would bring the courts into disrepute. Civil libertarians of all shades of political opinion debated the right of the state to impose treatment on supposedly responsible citizens. The favoured alternative was the 'justice' model (see Von Hirsch 1976; Carlen 1990). Unfortunately, in the rush to renounce rehabilitationism, few supporters of the justice model seemed to realize that the 1970s attack on welfare in juvenile (criminal) justice was the thin end of the wedge as far as welfare in general was concerned. The advent of Mrs Thatcher's government in 1979 provided a rude awakening. In future the emphasis was to be neither on 'doing good', nor on 'doing justice', but on making money. In support of the new, monetarist social ethic, Prime Minister Thatcher quoted the parable of The Good Samaritan as an example for our times.

The special illiteracy which has marked press and political statements on crime, especially youth crime, over the last 20 years has stemmed from two basic tenets: that all lawbreaking is a product of individual wrongdoing, and that penal policy should be based primarily on deterrence (Wiles 1988: 162).

> The idea of deterrence was dear to the heart of the Thatcherite wing of the Conservative Party; it followed naturally from their concept of society as made up of individuals making choices on the basis of a calculation of probable costs and benefits. The belief in deterrence by this faction was maintained irrespective of any evidence to the contrary because it flowed from the ontology built into their basic political philosophy.
>
> (Wiles 1988: 165)

That ontology also has a strong retributivist element. Two bids were made to reintroduce capital punishment during Mrs Thatcher's premierships. As part and parcel of the same retributivist-deterrent penality, there have also been repeated attempts to toughen up the regimes in young offender institutions. In the early 1980s 'short, sharp shock' programmes were introduced with the aim of deterring young offenders from committing further crimes. Despite an official report that they were having no discernible effect on reconviction rates, the regimes were extended and continued until 1988 (Pitts 1992: 180). From 1988 to 1991 the ideological emphasis was on 'punishment in the community'.

By 1995, after disenchantment with both community punishment and other provisions of the 1991 Criminal Justice Act (widely seen to be soft on offenders), together with increased folk-devilling of children and young people after the horrific murder of a toddler by two 10-year-old boys (the so-called Jamie Bulger Case), the punitive obsession was once more in the ascendant. In March 1995 a Tory MP called for the introduction of televised public floggings for convicted offenders. More soberly, the Home Secretary, Michael Howard, himself announced that certain existing penal facilities would be transformed into American-style boot camps where young offenders would be subjected to harsh, strenuous and deterrent regimes. Home Office projections released in March 1995 predicted that the population of sentenced male young offenders would rise to 7000 in 2002, from 5200 in 1994 (Home Office 1995: 1).

Overall, between 1979 and 1995, the emphasis has been on a retributivist penality *assumed* to deter. The efficacy of retributivist imprisonment was successfully challenged by Home Office officials between 1988 and 1991 and, for a while, the promise of cheaper (and more effective) punishment in the community was bought by a government whose very expensive prison-building programme has always been at odds with its commitment to a reduction in public expenditure. However, given the numbers of people already being punished 'in the community' by poverty and homelessness, as well as the many communities decimated by structural unemployment and the wholesale closing-down of industries, it is doubtful whether many of the offending poor could have taken further punishment in the community, or even whether 'punishment in the community' was ever really feasible. Even when criminal justice sentencing projects for young offenders have aimed at redressing some of the social inequities that may have made it difficult for them to keep out of trouble in the first place, they have been constantly undermined by market and welfare disciplines deliberately calibrated to make unemployed youth continue 'in their place'. Examples can be given in relation to both sentence feasibility and the welfare response to the needs of ex-prisoners.

There are two main reasons why community punishments are seldom feasible. First, because so many people are currently enduring domestic situations fractured by the pains of unemployment, low wages and poor housing. Second, because many areas of Britain are no longer provided with the level of public services upon which several community punishments depend. For example, while clients might be willing to attempt compliance with certain non-custodial orders, their probation officers might calculate that, given the tensions and frustrations already existing in their homes, they would be unlikely to complete any order involving constant home calls, curfews or house arrest. Similarly, officers might also know that while a complete lack of nursery facilities would prevent some parents from doing community service, a total lack of public transport would prevent other clients from getting to and from the appropriate schemes.

The punitive approach by welfare authorities to homeless ex-prisoners has also been well documented:

My client was staying at a hotel – she is now living in a homeless women's hostel. While she was in prison for three and a half weeks her clothes were stolen from the hotel. She applied for a Community Care Grant or a Social Fund Loan . . . The [Department] decided . . . to refuse her both the grant as she was not in prison for more than three months, and the loan because there was a break in her claim of more than fourteen days while she was in prison.

(welfare officer quoted in Gosling 1989)

At present no one is getting a crisis loan round here, even if they're sleeping on the street. The [Department] says they're not in crisis because if they've slept rough once and survived, then they're used to it and can do it again. The further down you get, the less you get out of them. People have given up. They think they've got to fill in so many forms, go to so many interviews and still not get anything. Which is what the government wants. They'll use it to justify further cuts.

(probation officer quoted in Carlen 1990: 69)

The new punitiveness

In 1992 Malcolm Feeley and John Simon wrote an article entitled 'The new penology: notes on the emerging strategy of correction and its implications'. In it they argued that a new actuarial penology is developing, one that focuses not so much on the management of individuals, but more on the actuarial assessment of aggregates (Feeley and Simon 1992: 449). Leaving aside the question as to just how new this argument actually is, what is certainly not new is the old structuralist argument that 'by strategy we do not mean a conscious and coherent agenda employed by a determinate set of penal agents or others' (Feeley and Simon 1992: 449).

Of course individual penal strategies conjoin to produce overall programmes which are independent and non-reducible to their individual parts. Because of the New Right's radical interventionism in criminal justice matters in Britain, however, it is necessary in the British context to consider the political agenda behind recent penal policy. What I am referring to when I talk about the 'new punitiveness' is the deliberate and comprehensive strategy of a government determined to punish a variety of groups seen initially as being either a threat to its own political power, or to blame for the failures of the economy. Whether or not the outcome was part of the original plan, the groups thus targeted for vilification have thereafter served as convenient scapegoats against whom to mobilize vote-winning law and order campaigns. Sure, the proclaimed policies have often been contradictory, and primarily because there has persistently been a disjunction between the ideological desire to cut public spending and the political need to whip up fears about crime so as to divert attention from continuing economic decline. Furthermore, there is little doubt that those involved in 'punishment in the community' schemes sincerely wanted them to succeed in their constructive objective of turning youngsters away from crime. None the less, by 1993 the scaremongering rhetoric had won out.

The Criminal Justice Act 1993, implemented in August 1993 amended some of the provisions of the 1991 Act and was accompanied by a large rise in numbers sentenced to custody.

(Home Office 1995: 5)

The disparity between the late 1980s official policy of reducing the prison population and the concomitantly punitive propaganda pumped out by press and politicians may well have caused needless sentencing confusion in the early 1990s (as well as being a waste of public money), but it also played a part in the maturing of the new punitiveness. Once it could be implied that 'punishment in the community' had failed (as it was always and already bound to, given that the programme was constantly being undermined by press and politicians), the time was ripe for a penal policy whose watchword could be explicitly enunciated as revenge. The triumph of the (in part engineered) failure of community punishments is that nowadays even previously liberal criminologists, politicians and practitioners propagate the (vote and grant-winning) gospel of being 'realistically' punitive. Accordingly, the only approved alternatives to prison are those transcarceral ones that promise to bring the pains of the prison right *home* to the miscreant in the community (see Lowman *et al.* 1987; Aungles 1994). In the mid-1990s it appears to be a penal stance approved by the majority of British media commentators, as well as by all three main political parties. The new punitiveness has three interrelated dimensions: the new politics of community penality; the new folk devils (i.e. unattached male youth and young single mothers); and the new politics of the crime victim.

The new politics of community penality is characterized by a privatized approach to community policing, a popular sympathy for neighbourhood vigilanteism, and a nightly TV parade of crime victims and their relatives demanding harsher penalties for *all* categories of offender. Even before the Criminal Justice Act 1991 had come into force, magistrates, judges and media were clamouring against what was being rather prematurely portrayed as a new leniency. While vigilante groups were formed and applauded for patrolling the parts that the police no longer seem able to reach, the government set about fashioning new and more punitive legislation. The Criminal Justice and Public Order Act 1994 abolished the right to silence of suspects and introduced new punitive measures against, ironically, those living most publicly in the community – squatters and New Age travellers. It also instituted some new and harsher measures against young offenders, including juveniles.

Davis *et al.* (1994: 10) vividly describe the widespread and much-publicized antagonism shown towards travellers during the decade prior to the Criminal Justice and Public Order Act 1994:

> there has been a growing call . . . for even greater powers to be introduced to curb the growth and activities of travellers, particularly new age travellers. Headlines in newspapers often use emotive and derogatory terms to describe new age travellers. Some MPs have also described travellers as 'parasites', 'ne'er do wells', 'scum' and 'vermin'.

The Act makes it more likely that increased numbers of evictions will occur, and that travellers will come to police attention ever more frequently. Indeed, under the Act,

The opportunity for new age travellers to live within the law will be limited. In particular, the children of new age travellers will grow up in an environment that is increasingly alienated from the settled community and their welfare will suffer dramatically.

(Davis *et al.* 1994: 17)

In fact, as Davis and his colleagues (1994: 17) go on to comment:

The emphasis of the [Act] is on control and concerns of public order. Such an emphasis oversimplifies the issue and reinforces the attitude that travellers are a threat to be contained and dealt with.

In relation to children and young people, the new sentencing provisions make fundamental changes in the powers of the youth court. Barnard and Bing (1994: 2) point out that:

Prior to the Criminal Justice and Public Order Act 1994 there was no power for a court to impose a custodial sentence on an offender under the age of 15, unless the offence was a grave one punishable with life imprisonment, or imprisonment of 14 years or more . . .

The Act introduces an entirely new sentence for offenders aged 12, 13 and 14 years – the Secure Training Order, and extends the maximum periods for which detention in a Young Offenders Institution may be passed for offenders aged 15 and 16 years. In addition the categories of grave crimes for which substantial custodial sentences may be passed are extended and the age group eligibility for such sentences lowered.

Allowing 'community' common sense to decide crime issues meshes very well with the New Right's anti-expert and anti-professionals propaganda. Although the rhetoric of punishment in the community quickly faded, that of treatment in the community (for the mentally ill) did not. In the mid-1990s, the myth of community treatment still seeks to justify the almost complete lack of care and shelter for innumerable mentally disturbed young people. Alone, destitute and vulnerable, they repeatedly drift in and out of trouble until, eventually, prison provides the only community care they ever receive. Since the passing of the Criminal Justice and Public Order Act 1994, it is likely that they will arrive there sooner rather than later.

The second dimension of the new punitiveness has involved the folk-devilling of young 'unattached' males and young mothers living separately from the fathers of their children. The 1990s attack on these young people was provoked by the mish-mash of anti-poor prejudices that comprise right-wing versions of underclass theory. Basically, the rhetoric goes like this: found in neighbourhoods containing large numbers of fatherless families headed by never-married mothers, underclass poor are those who, having been reared by permissive mothers and a supportive welfare state, now refuse to work and, instead, engage in predatory, violent, and society-threatening street crime (Murray 1990). Charles Murray portrays an underclass as being a special type of poor, unemployed people. According to him, an underclass is characterized by '[d]rugs, crime, illegitimacy, homelessness, drop-out from the job market, drop-out from school, [and] casual violence' (Murray 1990: 2–3). Amid the imagery of 'plague', 'disease' and 'contamination', his expressed concern for Britain is that the underclass will grow and grow, 'contaminating' whole neighbourhoods with disproportionate numbers of work-shy criminals. Consequently, violent crime rates will continue to rise. His proffered solution recommends 'authentic self-government' by local communities, with those not sharing the community values being encouraged to move elsewhere. Concern with the spatial control of societal threat and personal risk from disaffiliated populations is distinctly Durkheimian at the level of metaphor. In *fin de siècle* Britain, however, it has resulted in new legal and ideological refinements to minimize mounting (and guilty) fear of a youth citizenry whose basic citizen rights to work, welfare and shelter have recently suffered severe erosion.

The final strand in the new punitiveness is the rise and rise of the crime victim. Since the mid-1970s there has been a growing emphasis on the neglect and invisibility of the victim of crime in the administration of justice. The trumpeting of crime victim wrongs has been useful to anyone wishing to make an electoral appeal on law and order issues. Although at a common-sense level one might have thought that it is because crimes do have victims that anyone ever cared about crime in the first place, the 1970s rediscovery of the victim has certainly fed into 1990s punitiveness – and with a vengeance! The results? A greatly increased fear of crime, daily demands for stiffer sentences, and a steep increase in levels of criminological nonsense being peddled by press and politicians of (alas) all parties. However, when young people themselves are the victims of crime their victimization is seldom taken seriously, and they are more likely to be seen as protagonists who have brought their injuries on themselves. In short, destitute, able-bodied youth are as much feared at the end of the twentieth century as they ever were in previous eras.

The governance of homelessness

The economic relationships and political and ideological discourses conjuncturally producing youth homelessness were set out in Chapter 1. The regimes for the governance of homelessness are arguably as multidimensional as the conditions of its production. Just two dimensions will be discussed here: the *residential* (management of young persons), and the *legal* (regulation of the homelessness state).

Residential management of young people

Spatial aspects of social mobility and the management of contaminatory risk from a feared underclass (variously defined, but always posing a threat to those in the *over*classes) are addressed by Lash and Urry (1994: 168). More specifically, spatial aspects of lawbreaking have been of concern to criminologists at least since the pioneering work of the Chicagoan ecologists of the 1920s (Shaw 1929). The focus here, however, is not so much upon the spatial aspects of poverty, homelessness or crime, but rather upon the social significance of *residence* – as protection; as welfare distribution point; as security control for credit and insurance management; as both symbol of respectability and collateral for civil and criminal justice obligations; and as a disciplinary and surveillatory force, that from time to time gets more or less drawn into the state regulatory apparatuses.

Residential protection is of paramount importance to people unable to look after themselves. Traditionally, folk in need of such protection have been assumed to be those who through age or disability have been deemed incapable of living totally independently. In the case of young people in Britain, the age at which they may live independently has been set by statute, and as Cathy Newman (1989: 40) and others (Stein *et al.* 1994: 3–6) have explained, any projects set up to assist runaway children find themselves working within a very grey area of the law.

> The legal position regarding any under-16-year-old who wants to leave home is that they must apply through formal court proceedings under the Children Act 1989, to substitute parental control with that of another acceptable adult who can take parental responsibility for them. Young people under the age of 16 who have run away from home or substitute care are left in a 'vacuum' as far as statutory support is concerned: they cannot receive welfare benefits; they should be in full-time education; they are legally unable to work; they are not entitled to a Youth Training place; and they cannot enter into contracts to obtain independent accommodation.
>
> (Stein *et al.* 1994: 4)

> Legally, both 16 and 17-year-olds can leave home with their parents' consent. The position is less clear regarding those who choose to leave without parental consent. Police directives state that all young people under the age of 18 who are reported as missing must be returned to their parents . . . in practice, police officers use their discretion, and do not always return 17-year-olds who do not appear to be at risk.
>
> (Newman 1989: 6)

Since 1985 the Children's Society has been running a number of 'street projects' providing refuge for runaways, and Section 51 of the 1989 Children Act allows certificated refuges exemption from Section 49 under which penalties could be incurred for keeping a child away from a 'responsible person'. However, because of a continuing suspicion that they will be turned over to the police and then returned to parents or local authority care (a suspicion not totally unfounded in the case of 'non-refuge' agencies), many young runaways will not go near any place that smacks of officialdom. Thus, ironically, the very legislation set up to protect very young people can, under certain circumstances, make them even more vulnerable to exploitation, and in the long run criminalization (see Carlen 1988).

From its inception, the welfare state has favoured the family as the conventional unit for the calculation of welfare need and entitlements, though in more recent times the single person household has increasingly been seen as acceptable. Either way, the residential address has become the major (and for the techno-bureaux the most convenient) distributional point of reference, accountability and delivery for welfare and tax assessments. Therefore, when residents leave households that have previously been deemed relevant to the calculation of their benefits (or taxes), there often follows a transitional period during which recalculations of their entitlements are made. Not infrequently, claimants suffer hardship at such times, especially if they are young and homeless. This 'residential' factor in state welfare has persisted since the seventeenth-century poor law, and is, of course, partly a function of historically prevailing fiscal arrangements between central and local government.

As we have already seen, it can also have a disciplinary dimension. Arguably, the disciplinary relationship between residence and welfare has been unusually transparent in recent years, with media reports repeatedly seeking to shock by alleging a variety of so-called welfare administration 'scandals', including, for example: young people being able to draw benefits while staying in seaside 'holiday' homes; special provision being made to pay young people's entitlements when they are away from their usual place of residence; and special facilities being set up to pay benefits to claimants temporarily resident at various fairs, or folk, nature, religious or pop music festivals. Brendan O'Mahoney (1989: 34) claimed that social security departments in London were using deliberately coercive tactics to discourage young people from living on the streets of the capital. Enforcement of a residential discipline appears to have been the primary justification for the surreal routines allegedly employed:

> For those young people who are of no fixed abode, DHSS offices are nightmares. Many workers believe that life is deliberately made difficult for these young people in order to deter them from sleeping rough. There are stories of the young being made to queue all day, then being told when they reach the top of the queue that the place is closing, and to return the following day. Others are sent continually between local offices and the office at the Elephant and Castle that deals specifically with those of no fixed abode. There are consistent stories of the young being told, after days of this treatment, that their claims will not be processed for weeks. The young are admonished for being homeless and are told to return home as soon as possible. A wait of three to four weeks for a claim to be processed and money paid out is not unusual.

The experiences at local authority Housing Aid offices are similar. Young people are consistently told to leave London and return home as soon as possible.

Belief in the power of residence for disciplinarity and accountability is, in fact, so strong that whenever faith in the efficacy of penal custody has waned there have been numerous attempts to incorporate the power of domestic residency into the formal penal sphere as a means of strengthening its surveillance of criminals with domestic or family ties. Curfews, 'tracking' and electronic monitoring are all examples of the transcarceral campaign to convert the home into an outpost of the prison (cf. Fishman 1990; Aungles 1994).

Conversely, for outcast populations with no domestic or residential bonds, there have been, historically, a range of inclusionary schemes – from those of the early part of the twentieth century dedicated to taking youngsters off the streets into 'homes'; through the more liberal 'defining-in' pleas for real jobs for the young promulgated by Ralf Dahrendorf in the mid-1980s (Dahrendorf 1985); to 1995 proposals from businessmen in Manchester to entice the young homeless off the streets of the city's commercial heartland by first providing them with an attractive leisure centre and then bribing them with meal tokens to use it. Under the latter scheme, users would, of course, still be homeless, but it was hoped that their removal from the doorways and pavements would bring back shoppers thought to have been deterred from the area by the large numbers begging on the streets. (In fact the fall in trade was just as likely to have been caused by the early 1990s recession.) As this book goes to press in 1996 both major political parties are vying with each other in the stridency of their promises to 'clear the streets of beggars'.

A 'residential' qualification is required for voting; a verifiable address is necessary for getting many kinds of credit; and a 'fixed abode' is a desirable prerequisite for obtaining bail on criminal charges. A home address will usually be taken as indicative of the level of someone's income (or wealth), and in a number of situations a willingness to proffer an address is taken as collateral for any conditional trust invested in a stranger. In short, a permanent and verified address is seen as providing evidence that the addressee is both respectable and accountable. Increasingly, too, as less conventional forms of household develop, people in new sexual (and residential) partnerships frequently retain separate addresses (if they can afford to) in order to demonstrate their continued independence – and to have some security if the relationship should break down. With so much hanging on 'an address', it is small wonder that inappropriate residence (such as dossing in the streets, or squatting in someone else's lawful property without their permission) is seen as being a threat not only to personal safety and identity, to all kinds of property and to commerce, but also to the whole fabric of society.

Legal regulation and states of homelessness

The techno-bureaucratic and legal regulation of states of homelessness has focused on two prime managerial concerns: managing the incidence of visible homelessness; and managing claims to housing or doles based on a putative homeless status.

Management of the incidence of visible homelessness has traditionally been characterized by a paradox: when linked to individualized explanations of poverty, the prescribed antidote to homelessness has been supposed to inhere in income, the corollary prescription being that the homeless should travel in search of work; but, conversely, when linked to local or central state obligations to provide either alms or housing the prescribed antidote to homelessness has routinely involved injunctions that homeless claimants should return either to the place that has a statutory obligation to consider their claims, or to the administrative office best placed to process them (see for instance Henriques 1979).

Since the 1977 Housing (Homeless Persons) Act the main obligations to homeless persons have been placed on housing authorities (Hoath 1983: 7), and the authority in which a person is employed has a duty to house that person even when there is no other previous connection, e.g. of family or residence (Arden 1982: 6). None the less, criminal justice and welfare legislation, previous residence and employment status, as well as the politics, policies, budgets and ideologies of other public services, have all continued to impact on housing decisions and homelessness provision. Therefore, although the body of revised and consolidated legislation contained in the Housing Acts 1977 and 1985 (together with their codes of guidance for local authorities – Department of the Environment 1991, 1994) is the major legislation affecting homelessness in the UK, it should always be borne in mind that the implementation and effectivity of that legislation is also affected by selected provisions of the Social Security Act 1986, Children Act 1989, Local Government Act 1988, and Criminal Justice and Public Order Act 1994, all of which have already been discussed.

Applications for local authority housing on the grounds of homelessness are, in the main, processed under the auspices of Part III of the Housing Act 1985. Although its definition of homelessness is fairly narrow, it is not confined to literal rooflessness. The dominant focus is on persons not having anywhere to live, but it also covers anyone likely to be forced out of existing accommodation within the next 28 days, those who have accommodation to which they cannot gain entry, as well as those who have accommodation in which they cannot reasonably be expected to continue living.

Once a local authority accepts someone as being officially homeless, it has a general duty to provide temporary accommodation, assistance and advice. Beyond that, Paragraph 2.8 of the *Homelessness Code of Guidance for Local Authorities* emphasizes that:

> If an authority is satisfied that an applicant is homeless, in priority need and has not become homeless intentionally, *the authority then has*

> *a duty to secure that accommodation is made available* . . . The legislation makes it clear that the authority's duty to such an applicant is to secure long-term settled accommodation, commonly described as permanent.
>   (Department of Environment 1991; italics in original)

Thornton (1990) has argued that the 1985 Act was heavily geared towards providing for homeless families, and certainly only a very small proportion of young single homeless people have been accepted as being homeless under the legislation. However, the Children Act 1989 placed a greater obligation on both social service departments and housing authorities to provide accommodation for certain categories of young persons, while the 1991 and 1994 editions of the code (paras 6.13–6.17 and 10.22) remind local authorities at several points of their duties to 'young people "at risk" and therefore vulnerable by virtue of being homeless' (Department of the Environment 1991: 21, 1994: 25). Although the letter of the law might lead us to suppose that the Children Act 1989 would result in expanded provision for homeless youngsters, the national survey of social service departments by McClusky (1993) does not support any such supposition. Other (non-housing) legislation has had greater effect. Either it has contributed to an increase in young people's homelessness by increasing their poverty (thereby diminishing their financial capacity to pay rents or contribute to their upkeep in the family home); or it has made it less likely that effective provision can be taken up, even when the relevant authorities are able and willing to provide it.

Thus the punitive cuts in welfare triggered by the Social Security Acts 1986 and 1988 have resulted in the effective pauperization of 16 and 17-year-olds who do not take, or are not offered, a place on a Youth Training Programme. (For instance between April and September 1994, 40 per cent of young people at Centrepoint's Emergency Shelter for the newly homeless reported having no income at all – Centrepoint 1994.) Add to this the knowledge that not only has it been very difficult for homeless youngsters offered accommodation to get any financial aid towards furnishing and moving-in costs since the 1988 implementation of the Social Security Act 1986, and, moreover, that streetwise young people are well aware of the lore and lexicon of agency-maintained homelessness described below, and it ceases to be surprising that so many young homeless do not bother to seek accommodation from their local authorities. Yet, when they attempt to resist homelessness by squatting, 'travelling', or merely sleeping rough, they apparently cause such affront to conventional modes of living that they are very likely to fall foul of the criminal law in the form of the Vagrancy Acts and/or the Criminal Justice and Public Order Act 1994, already discussed above. The majority of young homeless people, however, giving no trouble to anyone and only sporadically subject to hostile media and police surveillance, are nowadays accommodated when roofless as very familiar outcasts on the streets where they live . . . and sometimes die.

Legality, lore and lexicon in the agency-maintenance of youth homelessness

Related to both the structural and precipitating primary causes of youth homelessness (discussed in Chapter 1) are the secondary, agency-maintained causes, the two foremost being the ways in which local housing authorities, their agents or delegates choose to interpret and/or fulfil their duties under the Housing Acts 1985 and 1988, the Children Act 1989, and the Social Security Acts 1986 and 1988; and the exclusionary categorization and referral procedures adopted by hostel staff intent on maintaining disciplinarity and 'quality' controls within their own hostels and professions.

Once young people define themselves as homeless, whether they then get safe and secure permanent accommodation through a local authority depends on three main factors:

- whether or not they apply to the local housing authority to be accepted as homeless;
- how the local housing authority categorizes their application, i.e. whether they are accepted as being homeless, in priority need and not intentionally homeless;
- how the local housing authority interprets its duties to people accepted as being homeless under the Housing Act 1985, Part III.

The above three factors are interrelated. Agency-maintained homelessness refers not to official claims that as a result of the scarcity of cheap housing many local authorities cannot adequately fulfil their statutory obligation to most young single homeless people at the present time. The term refers, instead, to bureaucratic or professional procedures for the governance of homelessness which *deter* people from defining themselves as homeless; *deny* that homelessness claims are justifiable under the legislation; or *discipline* the officially-defined homeless into rapidly withdrawing their claims to homeless status. Take, for instance, the pragmatic practices of deterrence, denial and disciplinarity engaged in by housing authorities as, in conditions of affordable housing scarcity, they attempt to allocate homes according to lawful 'need'. Insofar as the routines of deterrence, denial and discipline *mask* the amount of homelessness in an area and thereby enable housing authorities to claim that they are discharging their statutory duties (without actually housing the majority of young single homeless people at all) they contribute to agency-maintained homelessness (see also McClusky 1993).

The analysis of agency-maintained homelessness which follows is divided into three parts. The first focuses on the local governance of homelessness by housing authorities. The second describes the quality assurance devices whereby hostel staff maintain professional control over the selection and management of hostel populations at the same time as achieving the concomitant conversion of homelessness into something more amenable to professional social-work intervention. Finally, the third part discusses the contemporary role of agency-maintained homelessness in the regulation of chronic social change via the creation and subsequent deterrence, denial and disciplining of challenging populations. The main argument is that at the end of the twentieth century in England the management of homelessness is not merely about housing scarcity but has also become a site of struggle over social change.

Law and local authorities

A major point of agreement in the homelessness literature is that there is no generally accepted definition of homelessness. Greve (1991) suggests that the main reason for this is that the definition adopted has clear policy implications. There has been a noticeable reluctance for local authorities to employ a broad definition of homelessness as this would require them to accept greater responsibility for housing the homeless. Relatedly, recent research indicates that it certainly cannot be assumed that the official definitions proffered in the legislation (Housing Act 1985, Part III) and guidelines (Department of Environment 1994) receive uniform interpretation from the various housing authorities, agencies and agents routinely called upon to make housing allocation decisions (see Thornton 1990; Carlen and Wardhaugh 1992; McCluskey 1993).

The narrowest possible definition of homelessness is that of literal rooflessness, the total lack of any shelter. According to Dibblin (1991) the literal definition is the one which has been most favoured by government ministers in recent years. As we saw above, the statutory definition (Housing Act 1985, Part III) includes those likely to become homeless within the next 28 days, those who have accommodation but cannot gain entry to it, and those who have accommodation in which they cannot reasonably be expected to continue living.

Once persons have been officially accepted as being homeless, local authorities have a general duty to provide temporary accommodation, assistance and advice. Additionally, if assessors are also satisfied that claimants are in priority need and not intentionally homeless, authorities have a further obligation – to provide them with permanent accommodation. The *Homelessness Code of Guidance for Local Authorities* 'gives guidance on how authorities might discharge their duties and apply the various statutory criteria in practice' (Department of the Environment 1994: 5). Yet however much guidance is given, housing authorities, their agents and their delegates have inevitably to exercise discretion over innumerable decisions as to whether or not a person's circumstances match up to the guidelines – for instance, whether or not it is 'reasonable' for someone to continue to live in existing accommodation; or whether or not a person's homelessness is intentional, to give but two examples. In conditions of severe shortage of affordable housing and hostel places, local authorities, in combination with a variety of professionals involved with homelessness, have developed a very fine interdisciplinary mesh for the deterrence and denial of homelessness and the disciplining of the homeless. Such creative and coercive interdisciplinary accounting has resulted in the manufacture of an agency-maintained homelessness which, at its moment of birth, is either rendered invisible or translated into something other than it is.

The young and single hidden homeless are comprised of all those who apply to their housing authorities and are not accepted as being homeless (i.e. at least twice as many as are accepted according to Greve 1991: 12), together with all those who might reasonably be expected to have homelessness status conferred upon them under the provisions of the legislation, but who never apply (possibly over twice as many again – see Carlen and Wardhaugh 1992: 31). The major deterrents against young and single people approaching their local authorities and claiming to be homeless are:

1 the stigmatizing language of 'priority need' which in itself implies that the truly homeless are people who, in addition to their homelessness, necessarily have something else amiss with their lives;
2 the ever-more restrictive definitions of priority need employed by housing authorities pragmatically holding down housing demand to the level of supply; and
3 the panoply of assessment procedures which either reject a high proportion of young single homeless applications or result in offers of unacceptable short-stay accommodation (e.g. supposedly short-stay hostels where the majority of residents are actually long-stay, middle-aged recidivist alcoholics or otherwise disturbed people – see Carlen and Wardhaugh 1992).

The 'special reasons' which define young people (other than those with mental or physical disabilities) as being in priority need are set out in para. 6.13 of the *Homelessness Code of Guidance*:

> Young people (16 or over) should not automatically be treated as vulnerable on the basis of age alone. Young people could be 'at risk' in a variety of ways. Risks could arise from violence or sexual abuse at home, the likelihood of drug or alcohol abuse or prostitution. Some groups of young people will be less able to fend for themselves than others, particularly for example: those leaving local authority care; juvenile offenders (including those discharged from young offender institutions); those with learning difficulties and those who have been the subjects of statements of special educational need.
>
> (Department of Environment 1994: 25)

So, young people can be homeless without being in priority need. Yet young homeless people themselves are not primarily attuned to definitional niceties. They are concerned with getting a home. It is therefore not surprising that, after having the distinction between homelessness and priority need explained to them, young people conflate the two and thereafter distinguish between themselves and the 'really homeless' – who 'have something else wrong with them'. Homelessness, they learn, is not enough. Word gets round the streets and the hostels about the near impossibility of being assessed as being in priority need, more and more young people are deterred from offering themselves up for homelessness audit – and the numbers of young homeless increase.

Arguably, the plethora of interview and paperwork procedures required of housing authorities assessing homelessness serve the purpose of adhering to the letter of the law *on paper* at the same time as subverting its spirit *in practice*. It has become a routine government strategy to attempt to cover cuts in public expenditure with a 'legitimizing' mass of paperwork (cf. Ericson 1994). It is a strategy, too, that has been widely employed to hide homelessness in the cities and the shires. To mark the shortfall between homelessness 'need' and homelessness provision, local authorities lacking the political will and/or the resources to attempt to combat homelessness have been tempted to substitute the paper-accounting procedures of homelessness audit for *de facto* accountability. (Other public servants in Britain – e.g. in the National Health Service, the universities and state schools – will also recognize the 'auditability rather than accountability' ethic imposed from 1979 onwards on all public sector workers by a privatizing government.)

The 50 single homeless people (of all ages) whom Carlen and Wardhaugh (1992) interviewed in primarily rural Shropshire had certainly experienced their local authorities' interpretation of the homelessness legislation as being a deterrent to further hope of local authority housing. Only 19 of the 50 (38 per cent) said that they had approached a housing authority as being homeless and in need of accommodation. The other 31 said that they had not gone to a housing authority because they 'knew' that as single people, council housing was not for them, that 'you've got to be pregnant or married before you get anything from the Council'. Even amongst those who *had* approached their housing authority there seemed to be confusion about how the system worked: only 9 said that they knew they had definitely been accepted as homeless; 3 reported that they had been defined as 'intentionally homeless' (in each case they had left home after family quarrels, gone to live with girlfriends and then had quarrelled with them); and 7 said they didn't know whether or not they had been accepted as homeless, they had 'just been referred to a hostel'. Only 3 of the 19 who had approached one of the housing authorities believed that the assessors had led them to expect an offer of a tenancy in the near future. The views of the others were summed up by one young man who insisted: 'They haven't got anything to offer – whether they accept you as being homeless or not'.

By implying that truly homeless young single people necessarily have some problem other than homelessness, the law and local authorities together manage to deter young single homeless from applying to them for accommodation at the same time as producing legitimate statistics indicating that young single homelessness is less than it is. This is also one form of denial of hidden homelessness. Another form of denial translates self-defined and explicitly claimed young, single homelessness into other than it is by arguing (variously) that:

1 the claimed homelessness is intentional;
2 young persons have no right to leave the family home and claim independent accommodation; and
3 the claimed homelessness is a symptom of another problem (e.g. drug-taking) and cannot be taken seriously until the 'other' problem has been dealt with.

All three arguments involve refusals to recognize and endorse the chronic changes in lifestyles, employment and household patterns which have occurred in the last decades of the twentieth century. As a consequence, young single homeless people in Britain are damned (and deterred) by the law and the local authorities if they do not have 'other' problems – and are equally damned (and denied) if they do.

Lastly, a third type of homelessness denial occurs via a *suppression* which responds to local concern about visibly roofless people sleeping on the streets by taking them into new short-term hostels without making provision for any permanent accommodation. The result is either that the short-term hostels become *de facto* long-term hostels or that the residents get moved out from time to time, forming – together with a range of others whose homelessness is denied – a classic revolving door syndrome (Pitman and Gordon 1958) between street, hostels, shelters, friends' houses, hospitals, other institutions, hostels, street . . . and so on.

But what of those who *are* accepted as homeless? Some are offered good temporary accommodation followed by offers of acceptable permanent homes. Others are not so fortunate and the validity of their homeless status is then further tested by disciplinary invitations to:

- *do time* – in a hostel for twelve months before being considered for permanent accommodation;
- *'do a geographical'* – by accepting an offer of accommodation miles away from the 'home' area;
- *demonstrate desert* – by joining a programme addressing what is seen to be the fundamental problem in relation to which the applicant's homelessness is only a symptom; and,
- *demonstrate seriousness of homelessness need* – through willingness to accept otherwise unacceptable accommodation.

In the Shropshire study Carlen and Wardhaugh (1992) found that many young people were not willing either to 'do time' in a hostel or to 'do a geographical' by moving miles away from their rural localities to a larger town or the West Midlands conurbation. One recipient of a Wolverhampton accommodation offer by Bridgnorth Housing Authority pointed out that the authority had formally fulfilled its duty – even though he himself had perceived the offer to be a non-offer:

Wolverhampton is much cheaper than Bridgnorth and that's the way this Council discharges its duty to the homeless. They make you an offer, you refuse it because you don't want to go miles away. But they've fulfilled their duty.

(homeless man sleeping roofless, suffering from epilepsy)

None the less, some housing officials and social workers thought that in times of cheap housing shortage young people *must* demonstrate desert (by joining a 'rehabilitation' or work programme) before they can expect to receive housing support. Reflecting on this, a Shropshire social worker regretfully observed:

We're supposed to help them 'in partnership' with housing and probation etc. But 'partnership' or not, if there's no more money or resources in any of the agencies, we can't help them. The benefit system for youngsters doesn't exist now and we're swamped by young people with no money at all. We now have to distinguish all the time between the deserving and the undeserving and have to say at some stage to people nearing 18, 'We can't do any more for you'.

Young people may also fail to demonstrate the seriousness of their homelessness need by being 'too choosy' about the temporary accommodation offered to them. Applicants who thus annoy housing officials and social workers by refusing to accept the unacceptable are likely to include: young women who fear that they might be physically, sexually or emotionally abused in 'mixed' (i.e. not all-women) hostels (see Hendessi 1992); black people and others with experience of being victims of racism (see Yapp 1987) or who fear ostracism by their own communities if they go into white-dominated accommodation (Carlen and Wardhaugh 1992: 99); and all those who (for a variety of reasons) feel that they cannot cope with the very diverse mix of people in some short-stay or open-access units (see Carlen 1990: 45–50). None the less, however 'picky' (and with good reason too) some homeless applicants for housing may be, hostile anecdotal examples of their 'choosiness' pale into insignificance when compared with the well-documented quality-control assessments made by residential staff intent on preserving their own and their hostels' professional identities and interests.

Professional lore and the maintenance of local placing and spacing discipline

All the hostels are so set on their definitions and categories.

(worker in a resettlement unit)

Within local hostel and temporary accommodation circuits deterrence and denial are almost inextricably intertwined. The complex exclusion policies of the various hostels and schemes inevitably lead to equally tortuous assessment, categorization and referral systems which further impede the delivery of an efficient service to clients. Given that so many potential residents have already suffered the coercive objectification involved in the assessment and classification procedures of housing authorities and the categorization and referral paraphernalia of social services, it is not surprising that a substantial number reject the assessing agency before it rejects them. A senior probation officer graphically described the deterrent effects of long drawn-out observational assessments of hostel applicants prior to their full admission:

> The waiting time and referral procedures for some of the charities are so complicated that it takes months to get someone in. For example, I once had a most difficult and disturbed young woman and she got an interview in London for a hostel place there. She stayed two or three days at their hostel and then they turned her down. But not before she had turned them down.

Hostel exclusion policies constitute a major minefield of obstacles through which referring agencies and homeless applicants have to pick their way when seeking accommodation. Yet the reasons for exclusion are not uniform but vary considerably between hostels. They fall into three main groups.

First, there are the definitional exclusions which occur as a result of a hostel regime being specifically organized for the rehabilitation of people requiring specialist help, e.g. hostels for recovering alcoholics will obviously only take people with a drinking problem.

Second, there are the status exclusions: relating to people's status (or not) in the criminal justice system, e.g. if they are not on bail or probation they cannot go to bail or probation hostels; relating to family status, e.g. if they are male, non-pregnant or childless women they will be excluded from a few hostels, but if they *are* women with children they will be excluded from the majority; relating to gender, e.g. many so-called mixed hostels prefer *not* to take women, especially attractive youngsters (see below); relating to sexual orientation, e.g. some voluntary hostels have in the past been reluctant to admit people known to be of homosexual orientation; relating to racism – Ferguson and O'Mahoney (1991: 2) argued that 'institutional racism is . . . prevalent in the public and voluntary housing sectors' (quoted in McClusky 1993); and relating to disability, i.e. hostel design or lack of amenity forces most hostels to exclude people who cannot manage stairs or who need specialist facilities to be independent.

Third, there are the behavioural exclusions, directed mainly against people whose behaviour is *so* bizarre that it can safely be claimed that it would be seen as evidence of some kind of abnormality by most people, but also directed against those with records of violence and people still abusing drugs or alcohol, or even aimed at past residents whose behaviour is not very threatening – just likely either to be provocatively offensive or to drive other guests crazy.

> People who are mentally ill may not be violent. They may be no trouble at all during the day, but then go round knocking other residents up at night because they are lonely. It's not very bad behaviour but it drives other residents crazy. Similarly, we have rules against racist behaviour and talk. Now whereas others have the sense to keep their mouths shut even if they *are* racist, sometimes the mentally ill don't. What do you do?
>
> (hostel worker, Central London)

Although the professional training of the rehabilitation specialists means that they will welcome homeless people with *one* problem, *two* problems is often one too many:

> One woman we had recently was a drug user *and* mentally ill. Drug places didn't want her because she was mentally ill. Hostels for the mentally ill didn't want her because she was a drug user.
>
> (probation officer, Inner London)

In her evaluation of the Children Act 1989, Jacqui McClusky (1994: 4) argued that since the Act

> young homeless people are less likely to be accommodated than previously if they have the following circumstances: rooflessness, drug/alcohol problems and mental health problems. The assessment procedures are complex and inconsistent.

What chance for the majority of young single homeless people who start out with only two fundamental wants – a home and a decently paid job? What chance, too, you may ask, of grant renewal for any hostels which, by relaxing their exclusionary quality control procedures, fail to make out a case that they are still providing a specialist service for those at risk? In terms of marketeering morality, most agencies do not want to be seen as 'going downmarket'.

As with the housing authorities, however, so with the 'homelessness professionals' – denial via deterrent assessment, categorization and referral procedures is not the only form of homelessness denial. When transformational definitional processes fail to convert homelessness into something else, when exclusionary categorization fails to filter applicants into the next-door professionals' backyard, *then* it is time for 'reconciliation':

> For young people who have not been in care, authorities should always consider the possibility of a reconciliation between the applicant and his/her family.
>
> (Department of the Environment 1994: 25)

Maybe so. But some social workers inappropriately invoke real or imagined counselling skills in the service of accommodation-scarcity management, and attempt to convert young single homeless forced out of the family home into unruly teenagers who have merely had a tiff with their parents and now need advice as to how to make up and be friends. A Shropshire vicar who had tried 'reconciliation' was as dismissive of its applicability to the many cases of youth homelessness being daily brought to his attention as he was contemptuous of the governmental conversion of 'homelessness' into 'family breakdown':

> They [government/council] say that we should not be looking at homelessness but at what causes it, and by that they mean family breakdown. I don't see where that gets you in the short term. It's not much good when I have two young people sitting there and they tell me they've been chucked out of home, and I say, 'Any chance of making it up?' and they say, 'Not in a million.'

Likewise, an officer at a resettlement unit for ex-prisoners complained that:

> Women in prison are pressured to put their parents' address down so that's why women's homelessness is hidden. Women are not encouraged to say they're homeless. Three out of five young girls we had recently had definitely been told to put down their parents' address. Only at the last minute had the women insisted that they were not going home to all the problems they had before.

Many who slip past the gatekeepers subsequently reject the discipline of hostels and supported lodgings which impose regimes of surveillance and rigorous programming going way beyond the self-control usually exacted of people sharing living space with each other. Some hostels still insist on residents attending 'programmes', being out of the place for several hours a day, or being subjected to the counselling of the various professionals who can offer advice on everything under the sun – except, it seems, on how to get a secure and permanent home. Young people in supported lodgings too often find that landlords and landladies who take upon themselves an *in loco parentis* role become more difficult to live with than their actual parents were. Women who take the rubric 'mixed hostel' at face value, can be confronted with even more specialized disciplinary (and discriminatory) tests, as the male warden of a mixed hostel in Stoke-on-Trent explained:

> This unit has 16 beds maximum, including 4 beds for women – which are never full. In some ways it's good to have women because it can lead to the men cleaning themselves up. But young lassies can make things difficult. They fall in with one group, then fall out and go in with another group. I always explain to them 'You may be only one woman among 12 or 13 men' – and then it's up to them. But I warn them about falling in love; I say, 'You may fall in love, but then you may fall out of love'.
> We keep an eye on women; they can cause trouble.

In the Three Cities Project Sharon told us how being in a residential rehabilitation project had been: 'horrible, because I was the only woman there. The rest of 'em was men', while Bill added: 'I don't like to see women in mixed hostels – because there are sex offenders in here'.

Private landlords can pose different problems:

> In the private market sector . . . there is some trend to tenants losing their property as the landlord hasn't paid the mortgage. With certain private landlords the term 'deposit' is a misnomer; they see them as an *ex gratia* payment. One landlord, we could sue him in the small claims court, but he would only wriggle out of it.
>
> (Citizens' Advice Bureau worker)

> I was in a bed and breakfast. There were no rules at all. The reason more than anything is because it's run off the book [rents are not declared for tax purposes]. There were a lot of things stolen.
>
> (Josh, aged 21)

> I was told that the landlord was on the fiddle. Was about to be done for fraud, falsifying housing claims. So I was advised to move out of the house because sooner or later it would be boarded up. Then there was a fire there.
>
> (Lewis, aged 22)

> They put me in a hotel which was a shithole. I was sharing a room with this lad . . . sooner be on the streets. The rent was about £40 a week. The first room they showed me I turned down. Curtain rail, but no curtain. Window actually opened and shut, but the door had been kicked off, was all smashed up . . . and the room stunk of piss. I only stayed there two weeks, then I went back on the streets because I could- n't handle the place.
>
> (Carl, aged 23)

It is in the nature of the professional/client relationship that potential clients pose a challenge to the expertise, identity and authority of the professionals whom they approach. But young homeless people have a need which, in its essence, is not amenable to social work, medical or educational expertise. Homes for homeless people can only be provided by changes in political ideologies and social policies. That being so, the hapless professionals who find themselves confronted with young homeless people have either to convert them into objects of knowledge appropriate to the relevant professional auspices (cf. Ericson 1994) or to reduce risk to their own profession's image and authority by consigning the 'merely homeless' to some place else. If by chance any undesirables slip past the gatekeepers' gaze, programmes of discipline and surveillance ensure that they do not stay long. By thus managing risk and resources the homelessness professionals do their best under conditions of housing scarcity not of their own making. Nevertheless, professional assessment, placing and spacing procedures add a second layer of surveillance to agency-maintained homelessness (the first inheres in the law and the local authorities' interpretations of it). In themselves, too, these profligate categorizations create a new multiproblem population, 'the homeless', out of the thousands of young people whose one problem in common, homelessness, has initially been conferred on them by a radically conservative and punitive polity unwilling to confront old problems by endorsing and financing new lifestyles.

Homelessness lexicon for the management of change, challenge and conflict

Strategies for the bureaucratic surveillance and disciplining of the poor have become familiar focal points of post-Weberian analyses of mendicity, vagabondage, poverty and social control (Weber 1947; Foucault 1977; Cohen 1985; Adams 1990; Dandeker 1990). Foucault (1977) argued that one function of professional assessment and surveillance is the *normalization* of problem populations. In the context of homelessness management, however, it might be more appropriate to argue that today's young, single homeless in Britain have been gradually *abnormalized*. As legal and operative definitions of homelessness have become increasingly embroiled in battles over the forms and functions of the nuclear family, homeless young people challenging official discourse on the desirability of maintaining idealized traditional (white) household forms have been abnormalized by the legislative and bureaucratic-professional techniques for the governance of chronically uneven and partial social change. The changing forms and functions of the family in late modernity are marked by such chronicity, unevenness and partiality.

During the last two decades British citizens have regularly been subjected to injunctions from the political Right to return to traditional family values at the same time as there has been a rapid growth in knowledge about the high incidence of physical and sexual abuse in those very same traditional families. Widespread unemployment together with savage welfare cuts directed at unemployed youth have decimated family relationships at the same time as parents have been bombarded with professional advice about the importance and arts of 'good parenting' (Meyer 1977; Hall *et al.* 1978; Donzelot 1979; Rose 1989).

Unemployed youngsters who pose sufficient risk to become involuntary clients of therapists directing them to develop into the autonomous, self-fulfilling individuals beloved of postmodernists, routinely find at the local DSS office that they cannot even get their legitimate welfare entitlements without a social worker's support, status and know-how behind them. In short, although middle-class families in, say, Silicon Valley, California, may well find that they can restructure 'new forms of gender and kinship out of the detritus of pre-established forms of family life' (Giddens 1991: 177, drawing on Stacey 1990), for the thousands of poverty-stricken youngsters annually leaving either local authority residential care, or homes riven by conflict, the outlook is not so rosy.

In both the legislation and subsequent discourse on the legitimate meanings of homelessness, the major line of exclusion (of young people from effective housing aid) is drawn between 'unintentional' and 'intentional' homelessness. Young people currently falling on the wrong (intentional) side of the line are, arguably, all those who have left home without attaining victim (of some kind of abuse) status; have subsequently refused to claim victim status; or have failed to have risk status conferred upon them. But the line is not rigid. It is an index of constant struggle between those who wish to manage social change (and preserve for as long as possible their own favourable economic position) by maintaining the fiction that the benefits of nuclear-heterosexual familiness *always* outweigh the costs; and those who, knowing that the family-mongers are wrong, refuse to adopt, or, for financial reasons *cannot* adopt, the nuclear-heterosexual (preferably high consumption) family lifestyle. Consideration of some terms from the lexicon of contemporary homelessness discourse in Britain indicates that behind the laws and their activating lores there is a palimpsest of conflicting political and personal agendas, for each of which 'homelessness' has become the sign of something other than it is.

Priority need and intentionally homeless

'Priority need' and 'intentionally homeless' delineate the front lines of homelessness battles. Amongst single people, only pregnant women, adults with dependent children and those vulnerable because of age or disability are definitely defined by the legislation as being in priority need (Department of the Environment 1994: 23–6). Other 'special reasons' for construing priority need are given in the Housing Act 1985 and they mainly concern young people towards whom local authorities now have additional accommodation obligations under the Children Act 1989. In practice, the majority of young single people are excluded from the priority need category, while the eccentricities of the statutory definitions are underlined by the irony that

> single people who are sleeping rough are not considered to be in priority need [while] other groups can qualify as 'homeless' even though they are housed and are merely threatened with eviction. So you can be roofless without being 'homeless' and you can be 'homeless' without being roofless – indeed the title of one category is 'homeless at home'.
>
> (Gilmour 1992: 146)

Definitional and interpretive absurdities apart, the strategic rule for deciding whether a person who appears to be in priority need is indeed to be so defined is whether or not the homelessness is intentional. It is to the undoubted advantage of housing authorities with no spare housing capacity that the legislation leaves 'intentionality' wide open to the wildest interpretations which, in turn, can be made without challenge because 'the Act does not say that they [housing authorities] must have "proof" of the issues' (Department of the Environment 1994: 27). Thus young people thrown out of accommodation shared with parents, partners or friends can be defined as being intentionally homeless as can employees sacked from jobs with live-in or 'tied' accommodation.

The battle does not stop there. The family-mongers of 'underclass' (Murray 1990; Dennis 1993) and 'scrounger' (cf. Cook 1988) rhetoric have seized upon homelessness legislation as being one more example of the many ways in which intellectuals, feminists and the welfare state have together hastened the break-up of traditional family life (Dennis and Erdos 1992). As a result, when feminists like Beatrix Campbell (1993: 310) ask, 'What is it about cultures of masculinity that means men will not co-operate with women and take care of their children?' a deafening caco-phony of traditional family conservatives shrilly echo Thatcherite

> Norman Tebbit's saloon-bar erudition: 'if the state advertises that young girls with children for whom no father is willing to take responsibility will be advantaged in terms of housing and income above other young employed . . . there is a sharp increase in the supply of single parent families'.
>
> (Gilmour 1992: 149)

Risk and vulnerability

As with 'priority need' and 'intentional homelessness', so with 'risk' and 'vulnerability' – the legislation allows for a variety of interpretations of the priority category: 'a young person . . . at risk and therefore vulnerable by virtue of being homeless' (Department of the Environment 1994: 25). In practice, homeless youngsters seen to pose a risk to others by virtue of their criminal activities are much more likely to be offered accommodation than are their law-abiding counterparts whose homelessness is seen as being a risk to no one but themselves. A juvenile justice worker in Shropshire com-mented on the irony that many previously law-abiding youngsters find that once they have committed a crime the probation service can offer better access to accommodation than is usually available to social services, illustrating the point by adding: 'We had a lad who lived rough right through a winter before being placed on probation [and getting a hostel place]' (Carlen and Wardhaugh 1992: 88).

Yet as governments continue to displace the blame for homelessness from government policies and market practices on to social services (Chil-dren Act 1989) and other public sector agencies, so, too, they increase pro-fessionals' risk-awareness and desire to cover their own backs on the homelessness front. By competing with each other to procure and preserve what little empty accommodation there is for their own clients, the homelessness professionals contribute to a growing body of homelessness lore which, in proclaiming, 'No problem? No home', denies the equally urgent needs of all young people unable or unwilling to present themselves as being either risk-bearing or risk-posing victims.

Reconciliation

The obligation that has been put on local authorities to attempt reconciliation between a young person who has not been in care and his or her family adds further to the arguments that homelessness has become a prime site for the regulation and management of social change. While state-created 'risks' such as young people newly out of local authority care are to be contained in supported lodgings and hostels, young single people leaving home of their own volition (and without claiming to be victims of anything whatsoever) are to be persuaded to return to their families. Instead of the desire for independent accommodation being legitimated as an indicator of emergent adulthood and a reasonable aspiration of citizenship, it becomes yet another justification for bringing young persons under 'psy' surveillance (cf. Donzelot 1979) and attempting to arrest their transition into adult unemployment and homelessness statistics by returning them to childhood. It is a ploy that is often successful. Time and again during the Shropshire and Three Cities Projects young people in hostels indicated that they had been counselled into believing that they were 'not really homeless' because it was their 'own fault' if they could not live amicably in the family home. Thornton (1990) cites several pieces of research and official publications which suggest that the majority of young single homeless people have no home to go to (e.g. NACRO 1981; Barnardos 1989). Six per cent of women interviewed in hostels and bed and breakfast lodgings for a Department of the Environment survey in 1991 said that they had never had a home (Anderson *et al.* 1993: 104).

'Homelessness' and the 'homeless'

Struggles over the meanings of homelessness are not solely the province of housing authority bureaucrats and social work professionals. While campaigners against homelessness sometimes stretch the meanings of homelessness beyond semantic belief, young hostel-dwellers themselves call into question the categorizations imposed upon their accommodation status by contestants who appear to be fighting the homelessness battle way above their heads; and, moreover, in the furtherance of ideologies far removed from the concerns of an outcast youth-citizenry, already, and for the foreseeable future, excluded from housing, employment and all the other things that Thatcher's children were exhorted to go for during the deregulated 1980s (cf. Mestrovic 1991). Hostel residents interviewed in the Three Cities Project, for instance, repeatedly insisted that they were not homeless (because they had a roof over their heads, or did not take drugs, or did not beg), even though staff at the same hostels were equally insistent that they were.

Yet, although most of the young people interviewed suggested that they eventually wanted the security and independence symbolized by their 'own front door', they also frequently indicated that they aspired to a somewhat different type of accommodation than the one-bedroom flat envisaged for them by hostel staff. Fearing loneliness, financial difficulties and boredom, many of the homeless unemployed young people who have until recently been in local authority (or other institutional) care expressed a preference for a different type of secure, permanent home, one based on a more interdependent, less traditional, lifestyle – and not just for the short period allowed by projects especially established to manage the transition from institution to outside world. Sharon, interviewed in the Three Cities Project, had been in care and had never known either a conventional school or a conventional home life. Living at the time in a hostel with her 1-week-old son, she feared transfer to the flat for which, as a single mother, she was now eligible:

> They get you a flat, like, end of 12 months. But I don't really want a flat. I want shared or sheltered, cos I'm used to being round a lot of people.
>
> (Sharon, aged 23)

Having been already disembedded from conventional (but idealized) living via local authority care, unemployment and homelessness, many young people nowadays are unamenable to attempts by state agencies to claw them back into the morally and materially threadbare lifestyles of a society that cannot even meet their basic needs as citizens. From a slightly different perspective, Robert Lifton has described how people who have suffered and survived extreme victimization often conflate feelings of pride in survival with critique of the society seen to be responsible for the suffering. When this occurs, Lifton argues, survivors are often reluctant to buy into the society that caused their pain.

> In the case of the homeless ... I suspect that they're struggling to retain ... the pride of the survivor, the inability to form an alternative identity (at least rather readily), and struggling with a way of integrating their sense of being homeless and maybe their critique of society in their own way – however articulate or inarticulate it may be. It's like saying, 'I don't necessarily want to be just what you are. I may like a bed or a place to lie down, but that doesn't mean I want to become like you; and all you can offer me is the full package. I'm not sure I want the full package.' Something like that.
>
> (Lifton 1992: 148)

Instead of deferentially accepting the 'whole package' (which is usually a cut-price one anyhow) unconventionalized youth look around for new ways of living and the struggles over homelessness sharpen into battles about 'hippie convoys' and 'New Age travellers' (see Lowe and Shaw 1993). Indeed, Peter Marcuse has argued that the homeless shock precisely because

> The rewards of society have not proven attractive, or available to them. But neither have the penalties: jail holds no fear for them, humiliation, cold, and hunger are part of their daily lives . . . the system has come up against some limits it cannot exceed, has created a world it can no longer control.

(Marcuse 1988: 83–4, quoted in Wagner 1993: 10)

Travellers, single mothers, squatters and other folk devils

Homelessness has become an emblematic and archival site for the pinpointing of diverse social ills and multiple folk devils. (One of the most crass examples was to be seen in the posters of the National Canine Defence League which graced British Rail stations in Autumn 1993 with the arresting message: 'We have an answer to the problem of homelessness'. Only upon close inspection of the small print did the traveller learn that the concern was about homeless *dogs*.) Currently, the arch-folk devils of homelessness lore are young single pregnant women (in priority need of housing), New Age travellers and squatters. The Conservative government has threatened to bring in new legislation designed to deter single women (unsupported by men) from bearing children. Squatting was criminalized under the provisions of the Criminal Justice and Public Order Act 1994. Travellers are regularly pilloried in (so-called) 'news'papers more concerned with the profits of sensationalism than with accuracy. Definitions of homelessness continue to constitute and reconstitute indices and economies of spatial deserts. Battles over lifestyles and living spaces are fought out daily in Parliament, in the cities and in the shires, and the zones of exclusion are constantly redrawn.

Furthermore, if anyone still doubts that the governance of homelessness is as much about the management of social change and the denial of innovation as it is about housing scarcity, listen to the words of British Premier John Major at the 1992 Conservative Party Annual Conference. Having spoken against rising crime and falling standards of morality, the Prime Minister singled out New Age travellers for especial vilification, climaxing with: 'New Age travellers? Not in this age. Not in any age' (cf. Lowe and Shaw 1993: x). Yet as I type this in one of the most expensive areas of Central London in April 1995, I have only to go to the window to see three young people separately encamped in doorways, one of them begging from passers-by, two asleep. Prime Ministers and public may love to hate the threat of the travellers, but in 1990s Britain we have certainly learned to live with the 'the homeless'. As the twenty-first century approaches, they are an almost taken-for-granted fixture of both urban scene and rural landscape.

The accommodation of outcast youth

It is very easy when writing a critique of contemporary social ills to imply that everyone is out of step except the author, or, worse, that nobody but the author cares about the issue in question. That is obviously not the case with homelessness in Britain or the United States, or in the member countries of the European Community which has launched a research initiative to investigate social exclusion. In Britain there have been government initiatives to help the homeless; innumerable surveys have been conducted; the media have had a field day with 'homelessness' stories and documentaries; no end of research has been commissioned; and homelessness charities like Shelter, CHAR, and Centrepoint (to name only the three most well-known of many) continue with their painstaking work under political and economic conditions which must often be dispiriting. In discussing how 'we' have learned to live with (other people's) homelessness, therefore, it is certainly not the intention to imply that 'no one cares'. Rather, it is to raise and discuss the same complex of questions posed by Giamo (in Giamo and Grunberg 1992: 150) during the powerful interview which he and Jeffrey Grunberg had with psychiatrist Robert Lifton, and where he prefaced the discussion with a reference to the work of Kenneth Burke (1964; 1969):

> In defining humankind as the 'symbol-using, symbol-misusing animal' Kenneth Burke reminds us that humanity has the capacity for both conceptual regeneration and degeneration – the propensity to obscure as well as to illuminate. We have proposed that, in part, mystification (or the tendency to obscure) has gained the upper hand in society's response to homelessness. For example, despite the visibility of homelessness, extensive media coverage, intensive advocacy efforts, widespread volunteerism, government programs, and our familiarity as a people with this recurrent social problem, homelessness persists and an industry has grown up around it. How do you explain all this expenditure of energy with virtually no social transformation and none on the horizon?

Giamo was referring to the United States. But maybe a situation similar to that which provoked the questions there is even more astonishing when it occurs in Britain, a very much smaller country which formally established elements of a welfare state 50 years ago. For even though, as Greve (1991:4) points out, 'homelessness in Britain is not a new or transient phenomenon', the situation has been transformed in the last 20 years. Whereas homelessness used to be predominently a London problem and affecting families mainly, it is now much more widespread. It involves a wider cross-section of the population. The sight of young, homeless people begging in large numbers on the streets was not a feature of the big cities in the 1960s, not even in London. Then came the public expenditure cuts:

In the period of particularly rigorous public expenditure policies from 1979–1983, housing programmes contributed three-quarters of all spending cuts, and housing's share of total public spending, in those few years alone, was cut from 5.8 per cent to 2.3 per cent.

(Greve 1991: 40, referring to Maclennan et al. 1991: 23, citing Kleinman 1988; Joseph Rowntree Foundation, mimeo)

At the same time, and as we have seen, there were punitive cuts in young people's welfare benefits and steep increases in youth unemployment. News items on homelessness became more frequent, young beggars made their debuts on the streets of all the larger cities, and now, by the mid-1990s, youth homelessness is a fact of life or, as playwright Alan Bennett (1994: 182) has put it (though in a different context) 'the snake [has] swallowed the pig'. It seems to me that pig-swallowing, or more specifically here, accommodating youth homelessness so that it no longer shocks with quite the rawness that it did, has certain facilitatory dimensions. Five of them will now be discussed.

Enumeration and aggregation

One of the processes most commonly implicated in reducing the shock of the new involves enumeration and aggregation. Counting involves definitions, and the process of defining soon gives rise to debates about origins, characteristics, causes, authenticity, systemicities, probabilities, partiality and significance. Innumerable attempts to count or estimate the numbers of homeless have been partly responsible for the institutionalization of 'the homeless' as part of an aggregated index of social deprivation. Isolated (and disaggregated) on the streets, young homeless people may arouse a variety of emotions in passers-by. Aggregated in census and research data, they are more likely to be seen as part of a 'seamless web' of injustice which society is just 'not smart enough' to sort out (Kosinski 1992: 34). Another result of the aggregated homeless figuring in litanies of social injustice and discrimination in such a mechanical way is that 'homelessness' discourse becomes especially numbing. Repetitive and rhetorical reference to 'thunemployed (sic), ethnic minorities, "wimmin" and the homeless' discursively draws the sting of the very specific injustices associated with each of the differently-constituted but always and already aggregated populations.

Deconstruction

British playwright Alan Bennett (1994: 181) has described the

process . . . whereby terrible events are broken down and made palatable. They are first covered in a kind of gum . . . Then the event begins to be swallowed, broken up into digestible pieces, minced morsels . . . and so on, day after day, until . . . it will begin to get boring and the snake will have swallowed the pig.

Closely related to enumeration, indeed implicated in the very process of defining what is to be counted, is the art of deconstruction. Separation, sifting, classification, filing, translation and the archival (but partial) retrieval of discourses from previous eras (Victorian, in the case of the monetarists) are integral to the deconstructive urge. We have already seen how its artistry can be employed in the bureaucratic management of claims in excess of designated welfare budgets. It can also hasten the political re-education of those who have been slow to learn the ideological lesson that homelessness is always and already other than it seems to be; and it is absolutely essential in the psychic closing-off involved in what Robert Lifton has called 'doubling at the centre and numbing at the periphery' (Lifton 1992: 132).

Political re-education

One of the greatest aids to 'pig-swallowing' is political re-education – to help people 'swallow' things which previously they would have found unpalatable. New ideologies help, but force-feeding them to people by threat and wage coercion is often necessary in the short term. The dominant ideologies of individualism and free-market anti-welfarism have undoubtedly made it easier for the homeless to be portrayed as responsible for their own plight. In addition, many previously liberal social scientists, welfare professionals and left-wing politicians have also been force-fed into taking a more 'realistic' (job-safeguarding or vote-winning) approach to youth unemployment, youth homelessness and youth crime. As for homelessness, the following myths are still reworked by the press:

- there is a shortage of houses because teenage girls deliberately get pregnant in order to jump the queue for local authority housing;
- there is a shortage of homes because of over-liberal housing policies which have provided homes for people when they could quite well have bought their own;
- young people homeless on the streets are there because of a generalized breakdown in family life brought about by a 'welfare dependency' culture making it too easy for people to abrogate their family responsibilities;
- no young people need be on the streets, there are enough hostels places for them all; youngsters sleeping rough are those who spend all their money on drugs or alcohol.

And so on. The myths vary, but the overall message is clear; 'wet' liberals who argue the case of the poor on grounds of social injustice alone will either not be taken seriously, or the basic postulates of their arguments will be denied (see Cohen 1995 on 'the sociology of denial').

The only morality allowed is one which takes the bottom line of a bank account (state, local or personal) as its starting and finishing point. By and large, the young and unemployed homeless do not have bank accounts, they do not have the basic citizen attribute of an 'address', and most of them say that they do not support and/or will not vote for any party (cf. McRae 1987; and see next chapter). In short, the young, unemployed homeless have been excluded from citizenship. It is not to be wondered at, therefore, that they are sceptical about the efficacy of exercising citizen rights such as voting. A political re-education has indeed occurred, and it has affected people right across the class spectrum. In the process, the concept of the interdependency and mutuality of citizen rights and obligations with state rights and obligations has become somewhat obscured (cf. Dahrendorf 1985; Lister 1990).

'Doubling at the centre and numbing at the periphery' (Robert Lifton)

In an interview already referred to in this chapter, Robert Lifton (1992) argued that one way in which people can dissociate from the pain of being involved in troubling moral situations, is by engaging in what he calls 'doubling'. Politicians, officials and professionals whose work implicates them in (or forces them to witness) the persistent infliction of social injury can protect themselves from the pain and guilt that they might otherwise feel by developing a 'separate functional self' to carry out duties which as another self they would abhor.

This 'doubling at the centre' by those who have to act against their consciences is accompanied by a 'numbing' of sensibilities in those who watch from the periphery (that is, the rest of the population). 'Numbing' may occur either because people feel powerless and believe that they cannot do anything about the situation (this is where 'seamless web' aggregation helps); or because they may have answered what Lifton refers to as the 'ideological call to numbing'. (For instance, in the case of homelessness, they may have espoused the ideological myths listed above which put the blame for homelessness squarely upon the shoulders of the homeless.)

Lifton's application of this perspective to homelessness in New York is compelling, and it is resonant with messages for people at both the centre and the periphery in Britain, especially London:

> I'm struck immediately by how the homeless draw us into their plight, because they're here, they're around, and many people say in different ways that we can't avoid them. Even the Hiroshima survivors and the survivors of Nazi genocide could be avoided to some extent. They're out there. But you could call forth some numbing, as I call it, and it wouldn't take much to go on with your life and not be much aware of them. Of course we do that with the homeless, but we have to look at them. They thrust their homelessness right before us and they ask us for money or some attention – at least some of them do – and they're instrumental for making life in New York City more unpleasant. When people talk about why the quality of life in New

York City has become worse, radically worse in the last few years, I think it has much to do with the homeless and beggars. (They're not exactly synonymous, but they're close as anything else.) What that means essentially is that it is much harder to numb yourself to the plight of people who are hurting in New York. There've always been many of them, but they've been out of sight. They aren't now. Therefore, it's painful for people with any sensitivity at all to simply walk about and live in New York...it really means that all of us have to cope with more numbing, more dissociation, in order to live in an everyday way in New York City. And that's a very profound matter because it really means we have to become increasingly dissociated as human beings, as a society, as people who live in American cities and who like to live in cities.

(Lifton 1992: 131)

Institutionalization

So far the discussion has centred on the ways in which homelessness can be made palatable, explained away or bracketed off from agendas for immediate concern. Identification of all the aforementioned accommodative strategies, however, presupposes that the homeless do present a problem of some sort to themselves or others. In this final section, the discussion moves on – to consider how homelessness can become institutionalized so that it is *not* experienced as a problem (by some people) and so that both those with homes and those without them can take a 'survivalist' stance and say of homelessness, 'So what? I can live with it'.

Benedict Giamo (in Giamo and Grunberg 1992: 146) has observed that people who have survived any extreme deprivation, victimization or discrimination may take pride in, and become psychologically attached to, the condition survived. A similar state of mind may result in others who have had a raw deal being contemptuous of, and rejecting, the more conventional lifestyles of those held responsible for the social injustice experienced. Accordingly, they may then embrace and adapt the initially unfavourable conditions in which they find themselves; shaping them into new modes of living, into lifestyles more appropriate to their available resources. (New Age travellers may be examples of such survivor/refusers – as may also the other 'home resisters', discussed at the end of Chapter 1.)

Whether they thereby triumph over their oppressors or instead provoke/collude in their own further oppression is a moot point. What is more certain is that some of them sense that society's haves, as well as many of those who really have very little at all, may draw comfort from seeing the homeless on the street. Psychologically, at least, they can accommodate them. First, by seeing the homeless as both necessary condition and indexical baseline for their own fragile security; and second, by seeing them as society's 'designated victims', already so far beyond life as 'we' have known it that no further concern for 'them' is required (see

Lifton, 1992: 139–40). In a society increasingly conscious of multiple unknown risks (Beck 1992), at least the homeless on the street, immobile in doorways or silently selling their newspapers, are *visible* in their isolation. They therefore pose very little threat compared to, say, travellers or gypsies.

Beyond that they also have a positive function. So often have we been told that the market gives and the market takes away, that a hitherto unacceptable level of unemployment is necessary to bring inflation down, that the homeless on the streets can indicate to us in a very tangible way that the requisite sacrificial lambs are indeed upon the altar, that the market gods are being appeased. Even if people wanted to intervene, how could they when their own jobs have become so uncertain, when a generalized fear of risk and uncertainty, together with the prevailing ethic of individualism make it almost *immoral to care*?

And so the second victimization can occur:

> The homeless are like survivors who have what has been called 'second victimization'. And ... victimization in general entails some kind of imposition of the death taint on the group that is victimized. They are one's designated victims ... [M]any societies develop a designated victim, a group of people who serve them psychologically by becoming that and then the designated victim is as if dead ... it's easier to see them as death-tainted, as living dead or as nonliving dead, in some symbolic way because of what they've been through and, therefore, one can victimize them still further, *wash one's hands of them*. In various ways, actual or symbolic or by neglect, one can really thrust upon them a very powerful second victimization ... I see the homeless as having that happen to them.
>
> (Lifton 1992: 140–1; emphasis added)

3 |

SURVIVALISM AND HOMELESSNESS

> I've never got on with my parents ever since I've been really little. My Dad threatened to put me in homes and places like that and I always swore that when I was 16 I'd leave home. Me and mum were always arguing, and then one day we just had a big argument and that was it. I just said, 'I'm packing my bags and I'm going.' And so I ran away. It was the first time I ran away and for the first two weeks I was just sleeping here and there, wherever I could. I moved in with my friend for about two or three weeks, then into a hostel. I was living there for about two months . . . I went back home for about three days and it was just the same. The first couple of days it was like they were being really nice to me, trying to make it work. But then we had another argument. So I just packed my bags and went. And they turned round to me and say, 'If you walk out this door now you're never coming back, and as far as we're concerned you're not our daughter any more'. So I says, 'Well, fair enough then, it's my choice.'
>
> (Sharne, aged 17)

Same old story. Age-old tale. In Chapters 1 and 2 it was shown how political, moral and bureaucratic (including legal) discourses have, historically and contemporaneously, alternated in the definition and management of homelessness. At the same time, it was also argued that while homelessness in itself has been a site of struggle over social change since the sixteenth century, in western democracies *visible homelessness* has also perennially activated anxieties and ambivalences about the moral foundations of both citizen security (of person and property) and state legitimacy. Yet . . . and yet . . . moving away from the exotica of history to the mundanity of the present, the dominant contemporary concern about homelessness must be that now, at the end of the twentieth century, the conditions of misery, poverty and exploitation which the welfare state was supposed to abolish still flourish. In this chapter and the next, therefore, the everyday worlds of homeless young adults will be described in order to support arguments that were themselves developed from theoretical analyses of four sets of data: the history and management of homelessness as described in Chapters 1 and 2; interviews with 150 homeless young people between 1992 and 1995; interviews with workers from at least 110 agencies, projects and hostels involved with housing and/or homelessness; and the many previous studies of homelessness which are listed in the bibliography at the end of this book. All figures and percentages relate to the 100 young people (77 males and 23 females) interviewed in the Three Cities Project. The main arguments are:

1 that a significant number of homeless youngsters have had their otherwise mundane worlds so violently fractured by the multiple and interlocking effects of affordable-housing scarcity, unemployment and cuts in welfare provision, that attempts to survive and piece together their shattered lives *necessarily* involve a reordering of political, moral and economic possibilities;
2 that such reordering produces new modalities of living that are usually mundane, sometimes exotic, and often crimogenic.

In this book the totality of practices and discourses born of a reordering of the political, moral and economic possibilities attendant upon government-induced youth-pauperism and youth-homelessness is called *survivalism*.

Mundanity and exotica

Britain at the end of the twentieth century – and young homeless people abound. See them during the day meeting with their friends in city parks, libraries and museums, in cafes, marketplaces and town squares, in the day centres, projects and programmes specially set up to provide their leisure and personal hygiene needs – and also to keep them away from the tourists, the shoppers and those of us who may be offended by 'their' presence on 'our' streets. See them at night . . . at the back of restaurants in Manchester, beside heating vents and in public lavatories in Olde Worlde Bridgnorth, in shop doorways in Central London and rural Market Drayton, and at bus, coach and train stations up and down the country. Many have deliberately hidden away from prying eyes. They try to sleep in stables, warehouses, churches, dustbin annexes, garden sheds, the recesses of canal arches, underpasses and uninhabited buildings.

Late at night, and as the snow falls on northern cities, young people wait for the soup run. At London's Euston station early on grey mornings others prepare for the next move. Some will be washing prior to going off to work or breakfast, or to get some drugs; others will be meeting up with friends, one or two will be thinking of negotiating a bed on someone's floor before it gets any colder, a handful will be going for interviews with a housing or welfare bureaucrat, preparing for a day at college. A few, having decided to end their present homelessness stint, will be going home . . . to boyfriend, family, or even back to a local authority children's home.

The vast majority of homeless you will never see; they are those potentially homeless young people presently lodged in hostels or other institutions, as well as those hidden away (or squatting) in other people's homes or houses, encamped on someone else's land, without security of tenure and frequently in fear of eviction or a breakdown in the relationship with host or landlord. The only thing they all have in common is no secure home, though actual rooflessness is experienced as being such a distinctive badge of otherness and exclusion that amongst the most severely homeless youth – the young people who live on the streets – a culture of sorts develops. It is that survivalist culture – nearly always rooted in the mundane, often verging on the exotic – that will be explored in the rest of this chapter and the next.

Survivalism and leaving home

The majority (58 per cent) of young people in the Three Cities Project had lived with parents or relatives immediately prior to their present homelessness. Fifteen per cent had had their own independent housing, 8 per cent had lived with spouses, 7 per cent had been in prison, 6 per cent had been in the care of a local authority, and another 6 per cent had been living such a nomadic existence that it was impossible to identify a point at which they had 'become' homeless. Altogether 42 per cent of them had been in local authority care at some stage of their lives, and the homelessness of those who had been in care often began when, upon returning home, they found that they could not get on with families they had not seen for some time. These families had in many cases split up and re-formed, replacing parents and siblings with step-parents and their children. In all, 22 respondents had step-parents, and only 20 said that their natural parents were still together. A further 22 said that they had not lived with their natural parents for most of their lives. The family arrangements for the remainder had been so varied and changeable that they cannot easily be categorized. Conflict between the young people and their immediate households (whether consisting of parents, other relatives, partners, children's home, or 'other', e.g. 'supported lodgings') were the main precipitating causes of homelessness, with 54 per cent of interviewees giving 'family conflict' as the cause of their homelessness. The stories of the precipitating circumstances which resulted in them leaving home are best told in their own words.

Very succinct accounts were given of journeys out of care into homelessness:

I come out of care and I had nowhere else to go so I ended up in hostels. Didn't want to go back home cos I couldn't stand it.

(Tony, aged 19)

I came out of care and my grant got lifted and then I just went straight on the streets from that.

(Dominic, aged 19)

I rowed with me mum at first, then went into care. Come out of care, me mum died, had a row with me stepdad and went on the streets.

(Simon, aged 19)

The children's home was closing down and they were finding us all flats and they just couldn't do it in time. So I got moved into a hotel, like, and they couldn't fund it. They asked me if I could have anywhere to live, and I went to my brother's. Now he's in custody.

(Dirk, aged 17)

Once I could sort of properly leave care, I . . . got housing benefit and somewhere to live. It was a shared house. After a bit there was only two of us left in a five bedroomed house so the landlord just evicted us. We hadn't signed a contract or anything. We stayed with friends, travelled about for two or three years, come back to Manchester, and got a council place, but in a really bad area. So moved out of there to go to a private house, and the landlord stopped paying the mortgage, the bank repossessed it and we were out again. Another couple of years just moving about, and then got somewhere just after last Christmas. But didn't bother paying the bills and got really behind with the rent. Decided to move and the landlord got hold of us. Ended up in an alcohol rehab unit and that's where I am now.

(Jack, aged 23)

Many young people who had lived at home with their families had not felt 'at home' with them. Fifty-four respondents had left the family home because of family conflicts: 12 when they were taken into police or penal custody and parents refused to have them back; 10 because of sexual and/or physical abuse; and 6 when they went away to work. The remainder either found it difficult to decide whether they had ever had a 'family home' to leave from, or, if they had once had a place they called 'home', when and if they had actually left it.

I've got a family, and I'm of mixed race. I got adopted in a family and I've got three brothers and three sisters, and I've got another brother and sister out there of my own kind . . . and my mum and dad who've never seen me in my life. Everything started to happen bad when I left school. I was the black sheep of the family, and I started to burgle and smoke drugs . . . The grief started. I had to be in by 8.30 and in bed by 12 o'clock, and shit like that . . . I said, 'Look, I'm off'. I didn't come back for four days. My old man give me a smack, and I used to go to work the next day and think, 'Fuckin' hell! I've got to pay them 25 quid rent and the phone bill' . . . so after that I lived in the YMCA.

(Jock, aged 23)

Mum and dad never used to get on together, always used to be fighting. I think the reason was mainly that my dad kept holding her responsible for the way I was born, because I've got this disability. See, in our culture, because we're Asian, if you've got a daughter with a disability, it's like a big, bad thing . . . She used to take it out on me. I was made to do all the housework . . . It was pure hell . . . Mum wanted me to get married and I was really depressed. Suicide attempts started. I cut my wrists, I took a lot of paracetamols . . . I was so bloody pissed off . . . [Anne's parents took her to Pakistan where she refused to marry a cousin in a marriage arranged by her parents. On her return to England, she found that things went from bad to worse.] Then I decided. I thought, 'Right, I'm gonna leave home'. I was in a lot of pain, plus my back trouble, plus my anorexia, plus my bloody leg. But I was determined to leave home.

(Anne, aged 25)

Er, when me mum and dad was going through the divorce, er, me dad turned into an alcoholic. He turned to the drink so, er, eventually he was stealing and he was given 10 months in prison. And he hung himself in Brixton prison. My mum got remarried and I didn't really get on with my stepdad. My brother went in the army, and I was going with a girl in Birmingham (the one who's got my son). So I moved up here and slept rough, and then moved in with my girlfriend. Yeh, well, I finished with my girlfriend and I had to move out into a hostel.

(Eddie, aged 23)

The first period of homelessness was caused by a breakdown in my relationship with my wife. I thought it was down to me to leave and find alternative accommodation because there were children involved. I went through the Direct Access to the council accommodation of hostels. They moved me into a housing association and I think that lasted about six or seven months, moving between the two hostels. And I decided that the best course of action would be to go and find employment somewhere else. So I went to Europe and joined the Foreign Legion . . . Well, it was accommodation, wasn't it?

(Kirk, aged 25)

Money problems precipitated several moves:

I went to live with my mum for about four years – I was working at the time – and then I lost my job at the start of the recession. I couldn't afford to stay there cos she had to rent out the room to a lodger to pay the mortgage. So I left and started travelling around.

(Sam, aged 25)

It was getting really horrible at home. It was overcrowded and I wasn't working. Something had to give, so I had to leave. Well, they didn't have the money to put forward for me to get a deposit for my own place, so I just had to move out to the YMCA. It was chaos at the time. You'd be worrying sick, you'd be wanting to get a job, you've got to find somewhere to go. It was really stressful.

(Vince, aged 26)

Not all homeleavings were the products of overcrowding, the stress caused by unemployment, and/or the breakdown of family or domestic relationships. Several interviewees were clear that they had been kicked out because of their drugtaking or involvement in crime. Their stories will be told in Chapter 4. However, others had been physically or sexually abused before leaving. A total of nine males and 10 females claimed that one reason for leaving home was that they were suffering physical abuse there, while three males and six females (a quarter of the women interviewed) gave sexual abuse as the precipitating cause of their homelessness.

I was being sexually abused by my grandparents so I left home when I was 17 and slept rough on the streets.

(Wayne, aged 23)

The reason that we were all taken into care is when my sister was attacked. She was raped when she was 8. They never caught the guy. My mum had a big argument with me the day before and severely bruised me. So when they were checking out my sister, they checked me out as well. They found all the bruises on me and asked where they had come from. I just told them the truth, that my mum had done it. And that was it, then. We were both taken into care. Eventually I went back to my mum but that didn't work out and they put me in another children's home. I ran away, but my sixteenth birthday came so there wasn't a lot they could do about it. Then I got pregnant, and I had the baby. She was taken away from me after five months. I had started taking drugs . . . and every thing else.

(Tamsin, aged 17)

My mum and dad split up and my mum remarried. I had a twin sister, and till I was 14 we were sexually abused – from the age of 7. He just touched me in places. And then he started us on porners. When you get kids to do porners it's like 300 or 400 quid a time. So he was making his money! . . . We were taken out of the house and put into care. From then on I was a runaway. Just kept running away. My life was ruined as far as I was concerned, and still is to this day. So at the age of 14 I left the house and was living on the streets for two years, sleeping mostly under canal bridges, trees, benches . . . any place I could find.

(Dora, aged 19)

Me stepmum was sexually abusing me, and beating me up so I went into a kids' home. Used to run away all the time. Just couldn't handle being grounded.

(Tim, aged 20)

It started when I was 12 years old, when I started getting sexual abuse from my father. I went through police investigations, but they didn't have enough evidence, and my mum didn't believe it – he was my stepfather – so I went on the streets for four months.

(Fiona, aged 18)

I had to leave home because my stepfather was abusing me. It was either go into care or go sleeping rough where nobody could find me. So I decided to go sleeping rough, because I wasn't going to get all the hassle that me brother and sister got when they were in care.

(Sarah, aged 20)

Eighteen of the young people claimed that they had been kicked out of home, but the majority said that they had chosen to leave situations which they found unbearable. Moreover, many thought that they had made the right decision; they had achieved a control over their lives which they had not experienced previously, though Julie had found life on the streets so tough that she regretted leaving home:

If I knew that it was going to be as bad as it is – the situation I'm in – it might sound sick, but I think I would have rather stayed at home suffering than suffering out here. At least when I was getting beat up I knew I had a house over my head and clean clothes the next day, a bath and a meal. Out here I don't even know where the next square meal is coming from.

(Julie, aged 24)

A search for freedom was always a high priority of those who had run away from care. Others, like Anne, the Asian woman quoted above, had eventually (and sometimes dramatically) fled the family homes wherein they had been so unhappy. But other respondents had not been unhappy at home; they had merely wanted to do things differently. Rory, Sam and Mike were just three of several who liked the wandering life and spoke of a wanderlust born of a fierce desire for independence:

I didn't expect my parents to look after me. Got my own life and that's it. I left of my own accord. I usually travel during the season. The last two years I was in Europe, and I went to France to do the grapes . . . to Italy to pick the apples, and then to Spain to do the olives and the oranges. When I was in England I picked daffodils, cauliflowers, and I've done hops.

(Rory, aged 24)

I was living in a caravan. One day you're on the side of a mountain on a layby, the next you might be at the seaside in Norfolk . . . maybe in Derbyshire somewhere, travelling around. You can't do that with a house. If you bought a house, you're there for the rest of your life.

(Sam, aged 25)

I've got personal satisfaction out of it. Yeh, I've got my own stories, my own things. It's just part of the way I live, that's what it is, just part of travelling, homelessness is. You ask any traveller who has travelled extensively what he feels about homelessness and his answer will say it is part of the lifestyle. Me, as a travelling person, I did get a buzz out of it. I like going different places; I have money in my pockets, but not knowing, like, the unexpected. Like a quest, a quest I would call it; missions, going to a new town, a new place, or wherever. If you have to sleep rough, you have to sleep rough: full stop. It's like a challenge. You've got to do it to prove it to yourself, not anybody else, your self-satisfaction.

(Mike, aged 23)

People want to know what it's like being on the street. But I tell you something; since I've been on the streets I've been more happier. I've been on the streets in Birmingham, London and Spain . . . But I tell you something – I've had fun. I've had more fun on the streets than I've ever had at home.

(Sue, aged 17 who left home after being physically abused
by both parents)

Even though so many of the wanderers, runaways and hostellers argued that their own family life had been extremely dysfunctional and destructive to their personal well-being, what they had seen of so-called 'normal' family life had not enthralled them either.

Normal household? Normal families? No! No! It's better in a way being homeless. It sounds weird, but you get more help, and everyone sticks together. But in families you get none of it.

(Peter, aged 16)

In similar vein, others made it quite clear that 'normal' life, as far as they could ever envisage it for themselves, would most probably be routinely marked either by poverty, or, in the best likely scenario, by unremittingly hard and tedious labouring. So, as in previous eras, at the end of the twentieth century low wages, unemployment and a sense of despair about their life prospects again suggest to some young people that their best chance of survival is to go it alone, preferably keeping as much money as possible for enjoyment of the few pleasures available to them.

> If ya go into a hostel, ya got like £40 or £60 a week. Ya pay 60 quid out ya giro, and you've got £9 for two weeks . . . to live on! What ya gonna do? That's why most people say, 'Oh, fuck this. I'm not stopping here. I can't afford to'. Look at the money! If they're on the streets, right? they've got all that to themselves, ain't they?
>
> (Ralph, aged 23)

> I know people who are married with kids and both of them are working, and at the end of the week, this guy says to me that he's lucky if he's got £5 to go to the pub. You know what I mean? This is an honest, working man with a family and kids. Like here you get 35 quid in your pocket a fortnight – it's about 15, 16 quid a week. Then this fully mature grown man says to me, 'You're lucky. I'm lucky to get £5 to go to the pub'. And he's been working hard. But I think like, myself, some of the youngsters, teenage people coming up now, they don't want to just work nine to five, look after a family, get a pension, and die. You know what I mean? . . . It's probably that line of thinking that buggers them up from the beginning!
>
> (Roy, aged 23)

> It was a chosen way of life, yes. I could have stayed at home and got a normal nine to five, lived at home with my parents, been a boring old fart. It didn't appeal to me. I thought, 'I'm 17, but obviously I'm going to get older'. So I squoze as much into those six, seven years as I possibly could, and I enjoyed it. I can look back and say, 'I've done this, this and that'. That's the kind of happiness I like.
>
> (Mike, aged 23)

Agency and agencies

The reasons young people gave for leaving home, as well as their insistence that they had done the right thing in leaving, indicate that young homeless people do not see themselves solely or unequivocally as being victims of circumstances, even though most of them did feel that their home circumstances were so completely out of their own control that the only choice they had was to leave. Eighteen claimed that they had been kicked out of home, but the rest insisted that in leaving home (or care) they had been trying to take hold of their lives and make them better. Only a handful, however, claimed that since leaving home their lives had, in the main, been happy, and these young people were always those who, like Mike and Sam quoted above, had travelled around, earning their living by casual labour.

Seventy-nine respondents had slept rough at some time, though only 19 had never slept in a hostel. Except for the 21 who had always either stayed with friends or in a hostel, the most common pattern was to intersperse short stays or nights in a hostel with rough sleeping, staying with friends or relatives, or even returning home for a few days. All of them had contacted a variety of helping organizations, with the Citizens' Advice Bureau (CAB) coming in for the most plaudits (from the 23 who had consulted them), and the Department of Social Security (DSS) being almost universally reviled for what was depicted as being their most unhelpful response to applicants for benefits. A few respondents directed their anger at the impossibility of living on benefit payments – regardless of whether or not they had met with any difficulties at the local DSS office:

> I'm happy about having a giro off them every week, but even so! I can't live on a giro alone. I mean, £44 a week! . . . It's just not on, you can't do it, can you? I mean you've got money, fair enough, you can get a meal. But how can you find a place or something? That's why I have to come out and sit on the streets and beg for money.
>
> (Rory, aged 24)

> People say you don't need money to have fun. I'd like to see where that piece of advice came from.
>
> (Matthew, aged 18)

Young people coming out of care have to learn how to deal with the various agencies, as well as how to budget on slender means:

> Well, you try to get as much out of the Social as you can, and you just have to try and make it last. You just have to try and find ways round it. When I was first getting my money, I just didn't know what to spend it on, and I'd find other things would run out as well.
>
> (Kylie, aged 17)

One or two commented on the absurdity of the interaction between the rented accommodation market and a housing benefit system which results in highly inflated rents being paid to landlords housing the homeless.

> I went to Direct Access and they put me in a hotel which was £160 a week, plus £10 off me a week for bed and breakfast. Oh, there was a telly in every room and it was a beautiful house. But I just didn't agree with £160 a week. Even though I wasn't paying it, I still didn't agree with it. It's principle. Why should they get £160 a week for me to share a room with someone I don't know? A mortgage is only 40 odd pound

a week, so that's three mortgages. I could have been the owner of three houses! Do you get me?

I don't wonder there's so many homeless, because if that money's just going to private landlords for the bare necessities, then that money's being wasted. I'd sooner live on the streets than have that benefit paid to private people.

(Kirk, aged 25)

Most responses to questions about the DSS were characterized by sheer rage, as the young people talked about their battles (verbal and physical) for benefits:

DSS? I think they're a fucking nightmare. They'll be so unhelpful. It's like you're a burden to them. You're just another fucking statistic to them. I mean they're not very outgoing in saying what you're entitled to.

(Vince, aged 26)

The system stinks. You go down there, it's not your fault, you sign on the day you should have signed on, and they say, 'Three working days for your giro to come through'. And you're waiting the three working days, and it's the fourth day and you've gone down to get your giro, and they say, 'You're going to have to wait till five o'clock'. And you're kicking off about it, and there's no joy because, when you kick off, the security guard comes over, 'Please leave the premises because we don't want you to stay in here'. You can't win.

(Jock, aged 23)

The last time I went up I was really pissed off. I was only getting £29.90 every second week. Where does that get you in Manchester? So I went up and says to them, 'I want to know what's going on about my Social'. And I really freaked. I grabbed her over the table, and they got the Old Bill for me.

(Dora, aged 19)

Like a couple of weeks ago: I was sitting waiting for my giro and they said, 'Oh, you're late. Can't you come in earlier?' I said, 'No one's told me an actual time to come in. Don't talk to me like that, I'm fucking 24, not 5'. But they talk down to ya cos they got security, they're behind a piece of glass. Take that away and they'd be all nice to ya.

(Keith, aged 24)

Eighteen respondents were 17 years old at the time of interview, while three were only 16. As might have been expected, both because of their age and inexperience, and because of their non-existent (or at best precarious) benefit entitlements, the DSS experiences of these young people were often Kafkaesque in the extreme. They were sent from agency to agency, none of which had anything to offer them, and all were staffed by officials who protected themselves from the importunate poor with glass screens, security personnel, and impassable mountains of claim forms. It seems that in modern welfare bureaucracies the economically marginalized are always the wrong side of a glass screen, filling in forms and under surveillance from guards prepared to use strong-arm tactics against recalcitrants.

> I've never had any money since New Year. Something to do with my claim, opening a fresh claim, or something like that. Cos I'm 17 they want me to go to Careers. Right, went down to Careers. Careers said, 'No, you don't get a B1 form from here, ya have to go back to DSS'. Went back to DSS, right? 'I get a B1 form from here, don't I?' 'No, you have to go and sign on with Careers'. So I got pissed off then, ya know what I mean? Them sending me to back to Careers, and Careers sending me back to the DSS. So I fucked it off and came back here. And I've got an interview with them on Thursday . . . but it does your head in.
>
> (Ron, aged 17)

That Ron's experience was not atypical was confirmed by CAB and YMCA workers in Stoke:

> The biggest problem for 16 to 17-year-olds is that they've got no money. They rely on discretionary payments. If they're homeless they may well qualify for these. Even if they can find accommodation they can't afford it. For example: an 18-year-old single parent is rehoused in a flat. They have to wheedle money from the Social Fund . . . But if it's not 'exceptional needs', just 'homelessness', they don't qualify.
>
> (CAB worker)

Applications for any kind of benefits are all carefully screened and categorically staged – with the stages being renamed and recategorized as legislation or local conditions change:

> Sixteen and 17-year-olds used to be a nightmare in terms of benefits. Then it became easy, and now it's somewhere in between. They used to have to cajole young people onto YTS in order to get benefits, but now the DSS have realized that the YT places are not there. Young people still have to jump through hoops in claiming benefits: by going to the Careers Office, and by having a six week bridging allowance.
>
> (YMCA worker, Stoke-on-Trent)

In 1993 it was being claimed on all sides that the Children Act 1989 had raised expectations that not only could not be met, but which actually made matters worse:

> The Children's Act hasn't changed anything very much, you know. Social Services run seminars and they'll say, 'Don't expect anything in

under five years'. It hasn't made our job any easier; Social Services will pass the buck to the Housing Department. And neither Department seems to be being trained ... Soon after the Act was passed we took three young people to Social Services, and were told that it was a waste of time, they referred them to the Housing Department. Housing says it's up to Social Services.

(homelessness project worker, Stoke)

Wayne was 23 at the time of interview but he remembered what it was like to be just 17 and on the streets:

If you're homeless and on the streets at the age of 16 or 17, you cannot claim any money. They've got a thing called severe hardship. This is the way it works: if you're living in emergency accommodation you can claim severe hardship. You have to have a severe hardship interview every two or three months. Which is totally stupid, because that encourages 16 or 17-year-olds to go out to sell their bodies into prostitution. It leads to crime, cos they can't get any money. It's either prostitution, or criminal activities, nicking car stereos or stealing cars, or shoplifting. That's what you're going to have to do if you're 16 or 17. If you go into a Housing Department at the age of 16 or 17 and say, 'Look, I'm homeless', they say, 'Here's a list of hostels'. They won't do anything if you're 16 or 17.

(Wayne, aged 23)

People more experienced in dealing with the agencies were often equally despairing. Although they might boast that 'the more grief you give them the more [money] you get', they also recognized that 'with the Social you seldom win':

Ever tried getting blood out of a stone? It's very difficult. But if you don't get your giro, don't be angry, you should be placid. You expect to get your giro on a certain day; if it doesn't come, don't get angry ... cos it's your fault. I mean they can just turn round when they like, they can make you angry so they don't have to pay you. You know: 'I've instructed my staff that if you are offensive or foul behaviour, or threatening, they can turn like that on you.' 'Oh, don't pay this guy, don't send the giro out, we aren't going to pay him.' Next day, 'Where's my fucking giro?' 'Sorry, sir, it's been delayed.' 'I want my giro, so fucking get it.' 'Sorry, sir, we're terminating this interview.' Then they phone the police, and the guy's removed. So that's what they're like.

(Richard, aged 23)

Recognition that the welfare bureaucracies have a more pervasive and totalizing power over their lives than do the criminal justice agencies was most likely what made the homeless youngsters we spoke to much less vitriolic in their references to the police than to the DSS and the housing authorities. Though, as we shall see in the next chapter, many of them had had unpleasant brushes with the law, at least with the police they seemed to have had a greater understanding of the rules of engagement. This was not so with the welfare bureaucracies.

Endless form-filling demands put many of the young homeless at such a felt disadvantage, made them feel so often that they were mere playthings of the welfare gods, that several refused to fill in forms at all (or at least for the few weeks it took them to recover from particularly mind-numbing DSS encounters). All of the programme and project leaders told us how they had to help young people with their claim forms. Again and again respondents said how grateful they had been for this help. None the less, many also indicated that they felt anger at having been turned against their will into a welfare-dependent class without transparent rights to financial support in their extreme need; and dependent, moreover, upon the good offices of charitable organizations to make their claims for them. Barry's explanation encapsulates many of the feelings of other respondents who not only complained that the DSS was a deliberately mystifying bureaucracy, but who also suspected that form-filling was a device to represent claimants as being, contradictorily, both dependent suppliants and agency agents, as well as being both incompetent and competent players in the benefits claims game. In other words, young homeless people know that the wearying paper-chase for benefits is also a legitimating device which forces them to collude in their own regulation and disempowerment.

> I won't claim benefits [unless] Social Security will agree to sit me down and do it for me. They keep saying 'No. Get someone else to do it'. I'm sat there at a desk on my own. 'What's 20 minutes of your time to do it for me?' You know, they will have an interpreter if you can't speak English, they will have sign language for the deaf and dumb. Yet it comes to people like me, just basically can't fill forms in, because it scrambles my head, and they just won't help me. They just don't want to get the blame if they do it wrong, so they'd rather push it on to someone else. All your benefits you're not entitled to is then because you haven't filled it in right.
>
> (Barry, aged 25 and dyslexic)

Survivalism and hostel life

In the Three Cities Project, we expected talk about hostels to focus primarily on hostel rules and regulations. These expectations were not realized. Apart from routine mention of the stricter controls governing probation hostels, most of the young people we talked to spoke appreciatively of the hostel staff whom they had encountered, often saying that a particular staff member at a specific hostel was the only person they trusted. Even when they themselves disliked living in hostels so much that they did not use them very frequently, rather than blame the hostel regimes, they tended to mention either other residents or what they saw to be the essential nature of hostels as being at the root of their abhorrence of them.

It is in listening to hostel residents talking about their fears of other hostel residents that one can hear the first strains of the survivalist theme, the strains of which are never far below the surface in tales of the hostel and street-homeless. Its basic elements inhere in varying degrees of economic, social and citizenship (political) deprivation, to the extreme point where a totally excluded person has no access to any legitimate financial means and trusts no one at all. Most of the people interviewed said that they only trusted one or two people, and 13 spontaneously volunteered that they trusted no one at all.

Several young people said that they were scared of being in hostels either because they had previously been victimized in one or because, more generally, 'there is always trouble in hostels'.

In here it's terrible, because there's always someone breaking into our rooms.

(Jim, aged 22)

I've had clothes go missing; a pair of trousers and a couple of tops. When people are moving out next day and you're not there, they tend to just grab what they can off people and clear off.

(Eddie, aged 23)

Jock, a constant drug and alcohol user, told how he himself had stolen the fish and chips of another resident who had come home drunk:

Two occasions I clocked a geezer who came home pissed and left his tea on the table. When he went for a piss I ran upstairs with his fish and chips. [Laughs] Yeah, he went for a piss, wanted to watch a football match. I thought, 'Fuckin' hell! I've got a couple of spliffs in my pocket, got to get a munch before I smoke this spliff, and he's left fish and chips and a pint of milk on the side'. So I thought, 'Yeah, I'm having that'. So I went upstairs and yammed them one. He came back down the stairs and said, 'Do you know who's had my fish and chips?' Said, 'No, I don't know who's had your fish and chips'. It was me. Blatantly ate them behind his back.

(Jock, aged 23)

Matthew and Sharne, who had never been in any criminal trouble, feared that they would become implicated in the criminal activity or reputations of other homeless hostellers:

You're always with potential criminals, and at the hostel in Birmingham there was nine arrests in one week. Cos everybody else got arrested for all different reasons but I never got arrested ... But the dole money being so low, it [crime] is very, very, tempting, very, very tempting when you've got nothing to do.

(Matthew, aged 18)

I went for a job interview, and he stereotyped me just because I'm living in a hostel . . . Just because we're in hostels they think that we've either gone and robbed old people or broke into shops, or taken drugs or things like that. But it's not the way it is.

(Sharne, aged 17)

Others had a generalized fear of succumbing to a 'homeless hostel' culture of apathy, drugs and anarchistic and predatory survivalism:

Hostels are horrible crap. Just the people in 'em. Arseholes, a lot of 'em. They've got no respect for anyone. They think they've got respect for themselves. I don't like living in hostels, they're degrading.

(Mac, aged 20)

Hostels need rules. Homeless people don't respect the staff and they don't respect each other. Homeless people don't respect anyone. Out there, any place, they're on their own, they're an individual person. It's like having two arms and two heads; you're not a unit. If you're not a unit, you don't trust or respect anyone, and it's not gonna work. The residents bite back – that's theoretical talkin' – they complain, they fight, they smash things up . . . so it's like if you lived in the back routes of Cambodia it would be more civilized. But as a *place*, it's all right.

(Richard, aged 23)

You tend to get lazy. All you want to do is doss about all day, just sit and lounge about. Somewhere out of the cold, sit down and watch TV. It's just like with the drugs in a way, it's just a continual circle. It's like a circle going round. You get up in the morning, you get your money for the food for the day, just go and doss about, go back to your hostel . . . it's just going round and round.

(Josh, aged 21)

The majority of complainants, however, merely emphasized the obvious fact that hostels are not homes: privacy is hard to come by; entertaining and sexual activity is usually restricted and often banned; and hostellers do not have the degree of control over their lives that having an acceptable home confers.

Yeh, well they treat you as if you are a prisoner. It was for homeless ex-offenders. For *ex*-offenders! So they'd paid their debt. I couldn't conform to it. I was always arguing with them. Not just for my sake, but for the other residents. It was just a basic infringement of civil liberties – you know, saying whether or not you could bring a girlfriend back!

(Kirk, aged 25)

Under such conditions it becomes less surprising that many couples choose to sleep rough rather than risk loss of the only comfort they do have – each other.

You get no privacy in here. There's always someone barging into your room: 'Oh, I just want a quick word with you' . . . something about rent, and you're not allowed bags in your room.

(Mary, aged 17)

The rules in here, they are: you're not allowed anybody in your room after half past 11 at night, there's no discrimination against colour or religion, and there's no sexual activity allowed.

(Brian, aged 23)

You know, you can't invite your girlfriend up to stop the night, or cook them a meal, anything like that.

(Danny, aged 20)

We tried to go down the night shelter. They would take me because I was young, but they wouldn't take my boyfriend. They wouldn't take couples in, and we didn't want to be separated. They helped us by giving us blankets, but then you can't keep hold of them during the day. We used to put them in a black bag and shove them behind a hedge . . . and they would be gone.

(Jane, aged 17)

There's places that are for single homeless people, but they don't accept men. The point is: why should I leave my fella? I can't do that; I love the guy. We want to stay together. All we're asking is: 'Why can't they find us a place together?'

(Julie, aged 24)

Survivalism and living rough

When I was sleeping rough, anything could happen, like. You got no roof over your head. You don't know what person's gonna come up to you next. You don't know whether you're gonna starve to death or freeze to death.

(Ron, aged 17)

If you've got no money, you can't eat. You can't survive on water. You wonder what's going to happen. Who's going to come along. Is it gonna rain? Is it gonna be freezing cold?

(Spanner, aged 19)

The only people that you've got is the people that are in the same boat with ya . . . those are the people on the street. You gotta survive with your friends.

(Lance, aged 24)

You hear all this about streetwise. It's not bull. It's a big bad jungle out there. You gotta know where you're going, and where you stand. It's a big learning process, University of Life. I think that everyone should have a short stint of homelessness. I've got the knowledge to know that I could survive back on the street again.

(George, aged 20)

When you're homeless, you can't have people taking the piss out of ya. Cos if you let them walk over you you're not gonna end up nowhere. You're just gonna be a deadhead. If you stand up for your rights, they leave you alone. I can walk the streets now and know that I ain't gonna get no hassle. Well, ya get hassle from the drunks and pissheads, yeh, it's their prerogative. But people on the street, they leave you alone if they know you.

(Fred, aged 25)

No one knows their future, but a lot of people can plan their future. But with living on the road and being skint, you can't really plan your future. You just have to wake up every morning and make your earnings. Know what I mean?

(Rory, aged 24)

Survival on the street is a matter of keeping body, mind and spirit together. The body has to be fed, sheltered and protected against assault or exploitation, the mind has to be kept occupied, and the spirit has to be cherished sufficiently to sustain the young people's will to go on despite the odds against them:

How do I deal with it? I just get on with it. Just watch TV, just get on with it. I mean the next day's gonna come round, no matter what you do. I've been scared of reality for two years, but I'm still living in it. I'm still surviving. I'm a fighter, and I'll survive until the day I die.

(Cliff, aged 21)

New Street Station: I was walking down the stairs one night – there were two guys behind, and one in front. The next thing I knew, somebody with a knife round my throat, and, 'Give me your money'. Just laughed at him, cos I've got no money. I just took a tremendous beating. The way I see it, like, gotta take a beating, sometimes you gotta give one. That's the way it goes. Life is a circle, as they say. What goes around, comes around.

(Steve, aged 24)

You just have to survive. If you don't survive, you're dead, it's that rough on the streets. When you're sleeping, drunk people come and piss on ya. It's mad.

(Neill, aged 22)

The machismo of the streetwise does not protect against exposure to cold, hunger, violent attack and dietary deficiencies. In the Three Cities Project 45 of the 100 interviewees said that they had some kind of health problem. Of these, 12 had drug-related conditions, e.g. stomach ulcers, seven claimed to be mentally disturbed, five were suffering from physical injuries incurred during attacks on them and two were physically disabled. Other medical or (disabling) conditions mentioned were: asthma (9), epilepsy (4), arthritis (2), bronchitis (2), deafness (2), non-specific skin problems (2), migraine (2), cerebral palsy, leukaemia, psoriasis, sinusitis, and dyslexia. Three of the women were pregnant. Twenty-four of the 79 who had slept rough at least once said that of all the pains and deprivations associated with rooflessness, the very worst was the cold. Getting a relatively safe and warm place to sleep was a recurrent challenge:

The worst thing's during winter. You're out there and it's freezing cold and you just wanna curl up in front of a fire in some nice, cosy house. Underneath the underpass ... I like it down there. But when it's raining ya go along to the Fox and Grapes. It's got a big car park ... it's down there I sleep.

(Steve, aged 24)

I was in hospital a couple of months ago. I just blagged it for a bed. It was freezing and I couldn't be arsed sleeping rough. So I put on a little wheeze, went to hospital and stayed there overnight.

(Vic, aged 16 – asthma sufferer)

I've gone without food for two days, that hasn't bothered me. Cos the cold's hit me more than the hunger has. Most nights I feel as if I've been asleep for hours, but I've only been asleep for 10 or 15 minutes and I'm freezing. I've gotta walk around until I get warm, then park myself down again. But it's a case of up and down all night.

(Geoff, aged 20)

Berths were usually very temporary – for a variety of reasons:

Slept rough in a cardboard skip down in Tamworth. Great big cardboard skip. It's warm in cardboard boxes. I see the cardboard skip and I climbed in. I just threw all the cardboard over me and it was warm. In the morning I woke up finding something rockin', the skip rockin'. I opened the back and found it was about six or seven feet off the ground, about to be emptied. So I had to jump out in my sleeping bags.

(Ian, aged 24)

You get the lager louts out, that's when you get most abuse – mostly verbal, but I do know a few lads have been asleep and they've come along drunk and started weeing on them.

(Dean, aged 21)

We used to go to a place called Brown Street. And they formed the Brown Street Traders Housing Association, and got the police to move us on. Police weren't allowed to move us, but they managed it, you know.

(Jack, aged 23)

I did have a problem in the Bull Ring. I used to try and get in there cos it's warm, and there's chairs. The security guards threw me out. They pushed me down, ripped all me coat.

(Ralph, aged 23)

You're out there, people walk past yer. You sleep in a doorway, they spit at yer, try and set your blankets on fire, urinate all over yer. If we retaliate, we're in the wrong because we're homeless. They walk free and it's us gets locked up in gaol. We're protecting their shop, sleeping in their doorway, cos no one's going to burgle it. But they don't look at it like that. I don't feel safe. You have to learn to sleep with one eye open, one eye shut. Slightest noise you're awake. I've not had a good night's sleep for a year now.

(Barry, aged 25)

Getting food and keeping clean are also priorities, and these activities (along with all the business associated with drugs and alcohol use – see Chapter 4) are often as routinized as the lifestyle arrangements of people living more conventional lives.

I go for a shower every day on Canal Street, get my clothes washed. It's only 50p. And you got an iron, showers, shavers, soap, shampoo.

(Alastair, aged 23)

I used to get up at four in the morning before the farmer come out. He had a cold water tap . . . I just used to wash there . . . Or even if it was the toilets in the town, I'd go have a wash.

(Eddie, aged 23)

I wash in the canal, cos, like if you go to the coach station, they get really stroppy with you. They say it's for commuters, and, 'You can't come in here.'

(Fred, aged 24)

I go to Grosvenor Street Salvation Army for my breakfast and a dinner, then I go to Saint Augustine's church, get a butty, a brew there. That takes me up to about 4 o'clock. Then we go to Chinatown, have a few hours there. Then the handouts come out, between nine and half past. It's generally day centres we have to be in, because people don't want you on the street.

(Barry, aged 25)

Some people had a schedule of clothes-washing and bathing visits to friends and relatives' homes to ensure that they did not visit the same house too often; others, as we have seen, were extremely resourceful in tapping legitimate and free sources of sustenance. However, as legitimate sources of succour are apt to dry up at short notice (for example, when projects shut down because of lack of funding, or when an arbitrarily imposed new ban bars homeless people from further use of an otherwise public facility), the logic of destitution frequently suggests that illicit means have to be employed. Those less able to cultivate the macho image of the streetwise have to depend more on the exploitation of their sexual and social resources in order to obtain relief from penury. Julie engaged in prostitution, Wayne shoplifted and Sue and Dora had begged in order to provide themselves with what other people assume to be life's basics:

I feel frightened that come Friday we're not going to find anything. If we don't, we're going to be out there. We've got no blankets, what we going to do? Freeze to death? So that means I'll be out here trying to get money for a bed and breakfast. That's only going to be for one night. What are we going to do the next night? It's just like a big circle. We got nothing. We're doing it because we need to. We need money to survive. Without money and no food we'd die. Starvation! That cold thing, hyperthermia.

(Julie, aged 24)

Keeping clean? I used to go into C & A, rob a pair of socks and a pair of boxer shorts. Then I'd go to the swimming baths, pay me 30p, have a shower, put me clean underwear on, come back into town, go to Rackhams for the free samples of deodorant, walk out, and I'd be clean then.

(Wayne, aged 23)

It's actually harder being a woman and being homeless because a woman needs to change all the time, she's got private things to do, and sometimes you can't afford it. Then you've got to do something about it and you've got to beg.

(Sue, aged 17)

On the street, when you come on, what can you put on? You've got to walk round with bloody knickers, for fuck's sake. I know it's disgusting, but you've got no choice. It's hard, but out on the streets, you can't show someone your bloody knickers and say, 'Is there any chance you can give me some new underwear?' And you can't find places that'll give you free food. I have begged a few times.

(Dora, aged 19)

The greatest fear for both men and women was fear of physical attack and altogether 50 respondents had been victims of one or more crimes while they had been homeless: 15 (65 per cent) of the women and 35 (45 per cent) of the men, though some respondents thought that all women were more vulnerable than men:

For women, sexual abuse may lead to prostitution. Young women on the streets may be OK for a few days, but sooner or later they will experience some form of sexual harassment ... Like those sleeping rough in Hanley bus shelter, the men get to know they're there.
(worker in an accommodation project for young homeless people)

This worker's analysis certainly meshed with the experience of Fiona who had been raped while sleeping rough and who had previously left home after being raped by her stepfather:

I was raped in Piccadilly Gardens. I couldn't believe that it had happened. I never reported that. Just went straight home, got a shower, and went straight to my bed. It just brung back what happened last time. I'm scared to report it, just in case it happened like with my stepfather; well, it [the court case] just got flung out, there wasn't enough evidence.

(Fiona, aged 18)

Many repondents argued that being roofless is such a great equalizer that differences of gender and colour become less important than they are in more conventional circles – being roofless is equally bad for everyone:

Colour discrimination's got nothing to do with it. You could be orange with one leg ... because when you're on the street it doesn't matter what colour you are, you're still going to get shit.
(Jock, aged 23, mixed race: Iraqui/Scottish)

Leon (aged 25) thought differently:

I've been assaulted a few times mainly because of my colour. I find that the further North you go the worse it is ... I've had threats. When I've walked into a pub, then I know straight away I shouldn't be there. So normally if I walk into a pub and order a drink and realize I'm not supposed to be there, I drink up and go off. They don't have to say anything, it's just the attitude. They'll leave you till last to serve. You pay for your drink and they don't say, 'Thank you very much', or anything, just slam the money next to ya. You know straightway that's a hint to leave the pub. Cos by law they can't say, 'Oh, you can't come in here because you're black'. It's against the law, see. But they hint to make ya go.

Keeping body and soul together

As they talked of what it is like to be homeless, the young people ruminated almost as much about the effects of homelessness on their states of
mind, personalities, sense of themselves, personal relationships and views
of society as they did about the daily struggles for shelter, food, work, and
(in some cases) drugs. The image of the 'no win circle' was repeatedly used
to explain the contradictory processes in which they seemed to be caught,
and which were, in many cases, tearing them apart as they tried to make
sense of their situation, how they had come to be in it and what might
effect a change of circumstances. The major contradictions which troubled
them related to their sense of being both within and outwith homelessness, both within and outwith society, both within and outwith citizenship, and both within and outwith sociability. Thus, while much of their
talk centred on what it was like to be 'out there', there was also a reflexive
concern about what was going on 'in here', in their minds and their emotions. And they were not short of competing and explanatory narratives
to confuse them still further. All had come into contact with officials who
had defined, categorized and 'explained' them. Additionally, those who
were living in hostels often spent hours watching television – including
programmes on sexual abuse, institutional abuse, and homelessness – as
well as news about the enormous pay rises of the directors of the newly-
privatized public utilities.

More than any previous generation of poverty-stricken youth, today's
young poor are bombarded with images and parables of their 'difference':
a 'difference' which is usually portrayed in TV documentaries as inhering
in their conditions of existence ('out there') but which an army of therapists and other 'people handlers' none the less insist that they could
change if only they were to take a different attitude to life ('in here'). The
strain of living with and making sense of these contradictions was usually
indicated by talk of 'paranoia', and lack of trust in other people, though
13 spontaneously referred to serious contemplation of suicide on one or
more occasions in the past, and a further two had actually made suicide
attempts.

Within and outwith homelessness

All the people interviewed in the Three Cities Project were sleeping rough
at the time of interview, living in hostels for homeless people, or sleeping
at the homes of friends or relatives. Yet only 67 per cent considered themselves to be homeless, with 28 per cent not considering themselves to be
so, and 5 per cent saying that they didn't know whether they were
homeless or not. Given that about twice as many people apply to councils
as being homeless as are accepted as such (Greve 1991: 12), it is not surprising that in general there is confusion as to how homelessness can be
defined.

In the Three Cities Project the respondents who did not consider themselves to be homeless tended to be interpreting 'homelessness' as 'rooflessness', though in addition to pointing out that they had a roof over their heads, they often also referred to the fact that they were working or 'going to college', thereby indicating that for them the term 'homelessness' was encrusted with layers of other significations relating to (lack of) social ties and (lack of) social respectability. The people who said that they did not know whether or not they were homeless either referred to 'degrees of homelessness', or to the difference between themselves and the 'really homeless' who, according to the stereotype, are expected to have other problems.

> I was in London for two weeks and I went past Cardboard City. You look at them and you think, 'God! I could have ended up like that'. You're just glad that you're not like that and it makes you feel really sorry. I mean, you're still homeless, but it makes you feel how lucky you are compared to how they are.
>
> (Sharne, aged 17)

Vince had been glad to leave a hostel for homeless people because:

> (It sounds really horrible to say it) there were people there with mental health problems just been put in there because it's easy and convenient, people with drink problems . . . I mean, beggars can't be choosers, but you know! Jesus! Something a bit better, please!
>
> (Vince, aged 26)

Even amongst those who said that they did consider themselves to be homeless there was often a continuing sense of shock that the unthinkable had happened to them, an insistence that homelessness could 'happen' to anybody, and a spirited denial that 'the homeless' should be seen as either a homogeneous or a deviant population.

> When I weren't homeless, I had everything. I had my kids and I had a roof over my head. Reading the paper and seeing it [homelessness] on the news, you think, 'There's worse people off than them [homeless]'. But when you're in that situation yourself, you think, 'How could I have said that?' When I slept on the street it frightened me. I couldn't sleep, I was awake all night. I was just frightened someone was going to come and – you hear so many horrible things. You just don't believe it until you're in that situation. Until you're in that situation you *can't* believe it.
>
> (Julie, aged 24)

> People are always saying, 'It won't happen to me, it won't happen to me'. And the next thing you know is that it has happened to you.
>
> (Sharne, aged 17)

You know, you're working one minute, and then the next it's a bit of a slump, and then you're just back on the dole again. I mean there's people out here who want to work – and there are houses that are empty.

(Alec, aged 26)

Two years ago there was no way that I thought I would be coming to a place like this – no disrespect to it! But I never thought I would be coming to a place for homeless people. I had everything, good job, son, nice girlfriend. But – it's just like overnight – it's all gone.
(Eddie, aged 23, who became homeless when he left the home that he shared with his girlfriend, and then became involved in crime, and was currently on the run from the police)

I've always made my own decisions, they've been right, helped myself out of trouble many, many times. This was a good decision I made to come here. But my friends and family think I'm in a flat. It's not degrading, but it's not something you openly say to somebody in conversation. You know, 'Oh, where are you living?' 'Oh, I'm homeless.'

(Mike, aged 23)

I was only on the street for a couple of days, until I got my head together and went to Direct Access. I weren't gonna stay on the street. No way! Cos I'm too good for that.

(Cliff, aged 21)

Barry, who was dyslexic and was homeless as a result of losing his council accommodation after the death of his parents, was fearful of being on the streets for much longer. He did not claim benefits because, being dyslexic, he found the forms too difficult to fill in, nor did he beg or commit crime. To him the future looked bleak:

There's nothing good about living on the streets, nothing at all. It's not clever, it's not showing that you're a man. It's just showing that you're a total idiot, actually. I'm not knocking homeless people, cos I'm homeless myself. I don't want to live on the street for the rest of my life. A lot of the older ones stand in the alleyways talking to bins. I don't wanna get like that – not while I've got a hole in my backside. I don't wanna stand talking to bins. Know what I mean? . . . You get good homeless people and bad homeless people. Me, I'm one of the good ones.

(Barry, aged 25)

Within and outwith society

A second concern which surfaced in ruminations about constructions of self and society inhered in the contradiction between the young people's primarily conventional aspirations and social needs on the one hand, and the exclusionary processes to which they were continually made subject on the other. There was a general insistence that being homeless does not mean that one is anti-social:

> We just move among ourselves and make our own entertainment. You probably go to a night club, or have a night playing cards, rather than meeting in an alleyway – that's our entertainment. You don't realize until you live on the streets just how much you do rely on Society.
>
> (Barry, aged 25)

The image of the idealized Victorian Christmas was frequently invoked to pinpoint the time at which the most poignant meanings of homelessness are brought home to young people living on the streets:

> You see families going into shops, and you walk round and you think, 'Yeh, they're all right this year; what about me? What am I gonna do for Christmas?' You know? And you get really low. You see people walking round buying presents, all the family together, 'Oh, we'll buy one for our nan'. And you look round and, 'Nobody's gonna do that for me this year'.
>
> (Wayne, aged 23)

> The worst thing about being homeless? Not having a place to put my head down. And, like at Christmas, seeing families through the window, enjoying themselves . . . and thinking, 'And I'm in the cold'.
>
> (Sharon, aged 23)

Several had tried hard to get back with families, and others admitted to thinking about them, wondering what they were doing, dreaming of going back . . . and then remembering how short-lived previous reconciliations had been.

> I used to phone my mum and dad up and tell them where I were, but I'd already left there, so . . .
>
> (Danny, aged 20)

> Sometimes, I just feel like going knocking on me family's door. I walk there, just stand outside looking in. Just walk away.
>
> (Charles, aged 20)

As homeless youngsters begin to feel that they are more and more outcast, drugs and alcohol become increasingly valued for their social – and contradictorily, their anti-social – dimensions:

> Depression leads straight back to heroin. Gives you something to do during the day. Running round making money, you don't have time to stop and think what you're doing. It kills the pain in your head. You hide yourself from people and from yourself, as well. You start to have

a low opinion of yourself. People look down on you. You start to think, 'Am I that fucking bad or what?'

(George, aged 20)

They drink because it's society, yeh? Drink out on the streets! But that's our addiction to Society . . . I just want what everybody else wants, you know. A house, a family. It's not asking much.

(Bram, aged 24)

Yet people shun the homeless, and a mirror image of the difference that not having an address makes is constantly refracted back to them as the domiciled either gaze at them askance or scurry past with eyes averted.

We don't harm them, so why should they harm us? They look at you like you're a menace to Society. As if you should have been drowned at birth.

(Barry, aged 25)

People are going to work in the morning and you can see people sorta looking at you, giving you a funny look. You feel filthy.

(Leon, aged 25)

Worst thing? People looking down on ya. I can't help that I'm home-less. I never made myself homeless in the first place. I'm just one of those unfortunate people who's gotta live on the streets. I don't know any other way.

(Fred, aged 25)

To tell you the truth, I don't really care what people think about it. If people want to strike me off, call me a dirty bastard . . . soap dodger . . . dirty, stinking scum of the earth . . . Shit what they think! At the end of the day I'm living my life and not hurting no one else, so why should they poke their noses in?

(Rory, aged 24)

Everybody thinks that if you're homeless you've got some kind of problem – whether it's a mental problem, a drug problem or a health problem. There's a big stigma, definitely. And it's incredible that it's 1994 and this stigma still comes through. I mean, the whole thing . . . the way it's done on telly.

(Vince, aged 26)

Despite their defiance of 'homelessness' stigma, the young people recog-nized that it has real effects, both on the 'non-homeless' and on them-selves. To be seen (and to be treated) as different, diseased and dangerous does nothing to enhance self-respect. The looks of disdain, distaste and disgust which homeowners cast on the homeless are constant reminders of the social difference that homelessness makes. Then there are the looks of derision and fear:

> I love to work, but I am what is known as unemployable. You go for job interviews and people look at you, 'Sod off', like. I went for a job in Walsall, making concrete slabs. The bloke just looked at me and laughed. I said to him, 'Why are you laughing?' He said, 'Well, look at yer, you're an undesirable, basically'. I said, 'Well, if you look at the job, mate, what's the point in turning up in a suit and tie, cos you're going to get messy?'
>
> (Steve, aged 24)

> I was looking for work, and I couldn't get work. If you've not shaved and your clothes are scruffy you can't work. You need the home base. It does make a difference and it's a kind of vicious circle.
>
> (Mike, aged 23)

> It's not a nice thing to do, walking the streets and picking ends up. At the moment I've gone for three or four months without having a penny in my pocket. Sometimes, if they see you picking butt ends off the floor, they will say to you, 'Here's a couple of cigarettes. Don't do it, it's disgusting.' But you can't catch AIDS off a cigarette butt.
>
> (Barry, aged 25)

> You get up in the morning and you can't think, 'I've got to get a job', because you need somewhere to live first. It cancels itself out, and you think, 'Does anybody give a shit? Fucking hell! Am I inferior?' You do get paranoid. People do look down upon ya. You feel different about yourself all the time. That's brought on by being homeless . . .
>
> Then, a lot of the public get a bit nervous with people hanging around in groups. The general public get frightened. But they [the street homeless] usually hang around in groups for their own protection.
>
> (Vince, aged 26)

Within and outwith citizenship

Concepts of contractual rights, duties and obligations are central to modern notions of citizenship. Citizens have the right to participate in public life and a duty to do so according to the laws of the land. In return for citizens' observation of the rights and duties of citizenship, the state has an obligation to protect their private rights. The nature of these private rights is always subject to debate, but, it is usually assumed that the state will protect a citizen's person and property against unlawful attack. Under *welfare* state regimes it is additionally assumed that a citizen will be accorded some measure of protection against the evils of destitution, disease and ignorance (see Deakin *et al*. 1990 for a comprehensive discussion of contemporary citizenship issues in Britain).

The significance of 'citizenship' in this book is not as a lever for getting at whether young homeless people are being denied citizen rights, but as a concept of orientation to help illuminate analysis of the generalized feeling among the young homeless that insofar as 'Society' appears to have let them down, their own citizenship obligations are to the same degree diminished. The irony, as they see it, lies in the daily reminder from the law and order and welfare bureaucracies that although the state has little protection to offer young homeless people, it will increasingly use its regulatory and repressive apparatuses to ensure that the 'non-homeless' are protected against the homeless. It is in this sense that young homeless people are both within and outwith citizenship.

A constant theme in all the discourse of young homeless people is about the extent to which not having a permanent residence denudes life of amenities that are considered to be basic prerequisites for modern living. The roofless are denied warmth, shelter, privacy, and all the amenities usually pertaining to domesticity. Roofless homeless and homeless-hostellers alike admit to feelings of insecurity and fear stemming from either threats to, or lack of protection of, their persons and property. Additionally, they are denied all the welfare goods that are dependent on having a permanent address. The homeless, according to many of the regulations of the welfare bureaucracies, are outwith citizenship because they cannot be *addressed*. Without an address you cannot exist in a file, and if you have no form of address, you are a nobody. Thus in order to exist as welfare citizens, the roofless and the wanderers have to risk prosecution by giving a fictitious address, while, in order to get a job, the hostellers feel that they have to give a different and 'better' address.

> You feel like the community, the government, the council – whatever – have forgotten you. You're at the bottom and there's no way you can get out of that rut unless you've got an address. If you're homeless, you haven't got an address, unless you move into a hostel or shared accommodation.
>
> (Brian, aged 33)

> The 'Housing' [Departments] reject a lot of people. You got to have an address to even put in for a place of your own.
>
> (Joe, aged 24)

> Once you're actually on the streets, it's hard to get somewhere. If you've got an address you can get things sent there in the post. If it weren't for the *The Big Issue* [a magazine sold by the homeless] I wouldn't have nowhere to send my stuff. Cos this address I give to the council, for them to send my stuff.
>
> (Dean, aged 21)

If you're on the streets you can't get housed. And you can't get housed if you've not got any benefits. But you can't get any benefits if you're on the streets. It's like one circle. You can't win.

(Peter, aged 16)

If you're homeless, they [housing departments] send you for loads and loadsa interviews. Sometimes they tell you to find an address, before they give you . . . nothin'!

(Mac, aged 20)

I haven't got an address to vote from, so I'm not on the electoral roll. I'd like to vote. I think it would make a difference.

(Bram, aged 24)

You can't get registered with a doctor if you haven't got an address. If you ain't got an address, they don't want to know.

(Barry, aged 25)

If you are homeless, you don't get the rights that you can get if you have a home. I haven't got a home, so it makes it harder for my money to come through.

(Lance, aged 24)

You need an address to get access.

(Bram, aged 24, explaining why he no longer sees his daughter)

If you put the title 'Hostel' at the top of an application, 99 per cent of the time you'd be turned down from that work.

(Mark, aged 18)

I think people's attitudes change once you tell them you're in a hostel. They start up as if you was some ex-criminal or something.

(Kylie, aged 17)

If a homeless person gets in trouble with the courts or the police, being of 'no fixed abode' may increase the likelihood of a custodial sentence. But the most acute sense of grievance suffered by the street homeless inheres in their experience of being denied access to places that are freely open to the non-homeless. As they attempt to rest in pubs, public transport depots, parks, libraries and museums, the young 'no fixed aboders' are repeatedly harried by a variety of proprietors and minor officials intent on moving them on. Many of the people interviewed spontaneously mentioned help they had received from the police. None the less, as many again could recount tales of police harassment or of extra-close police surveillance:

Recently there was a lot of hassle in Piccadilly Gardens. A lot of my friends got arrested. Since then they've [the police] been going around looking for the rest of the people that were involved – stopping me and asking me my name and everything. Saying, 'We just want to make sure about the people selling *The Big Issue* . . . if you can tell us your name and address.' They're not allowed to do that, but if I just say, 'I'm not giving you my name and address', I'm gonna get loads of hassle. So I give them my brother's name.

(Jack, aged 23)

I was arrested yesterday. I was sleeping on a bench, just minding my own damn business. I was just tired. I was asleep for about five minutes: 'Come on, get up, get up.' Turned round, saw two coppers. He says, 'Get up.' I turned round and said, 'Hold on. This is not necessary. You can't talk to me like dirt. Please', I says, 'I'm homeless. I'm not causing any damage.' He says, 'You're sleeping on the bench. That's not nice for the people who're walking round.' I says, 'Well, that isn't my problem, that's their problem. Please pack this in.' He says, 'No, move, or you will be nicked.' So where does he book me? Stafford police station. Kept me in there for an hour, then took me out. At least I was in there for an hour. I was in a warm cell – quite happy! God! I'd done nothing wrong, so they had to chuck me out then . . . and they give me a cuppa tea.

You gotta defend yourself, and when you try to defend yourself, because you are on the street, the police think that because you're homeless you're causing the trouble. He got his fixed address, so there's an innocent man.

(Lance, aged 24)

The greatest indignation about police violation of rights was expressed by those who felt that in adopting a travelling lifestyle they had indeed tried to help themselves – only to be vilified by the press, and, to all intents and purposes, criminalized by the Criminal Justice and Public Order Act 1994, a piece of legislation which made it even more difficult for travellers 'to live within the law' (Davis *et al.* 1994). Andy expounded on this at some length:

There's counties where you could go and park up and have no hassle from the police. Now, you're just getting victimized. Shropshire is one county I've been through. The first three years it was fine. The last time I went there, there was mass evictions all round. The local newspapers were constantly going on about travellers. What messes they were making, and, 'Isn't it disgusting they're here, destroying our country-side' . . . and all the usual rubbish. There was a site near a school, so they put into the paper that people had to go and pick up their kids at a certain time, that we were going to steal them! It goes back to the old sorts of things that I heard when I was a kid, when gypsies were around, you know? And there's the Criminal Justice Act will change things a hell of a lot more, because it's gonna give the police the power to evict anyone, on the basis that if there's more than six people they're going to have a party. . .They say they are trying to help the homeless, and then what do they do? They change the law to make squatting illegal! You know, 'Oh, great! There's another ten thousand people on the street! Whoops!' They've made a large mess because they want to go back to some kind of Victorian standard. You know, basically two classes – working class and government's class. They don't like the idea of people being able to move, *and not being accounted for.*

(Andy, aged 25; my emphasis)

Within and outwith sociability

I've got depressed and isolated. I've felt disgusted. People thought I was a piece of dirt. Everybody deserves a life. But when you're on the streets it's hard because you don't know who to trust. You don't know whether to trust the Old Bill; you don't know whether to trust the people walking around you; you don't even know whether to trust the poor old drunkards. And yet sometimes they come and they flipping try to help you, yeh? But you go, 'Go away! Go away! Please leave me alone. I didn't do nothing to deserve this'.

(Dora, aged 19)

Interviewer: Do you get much of a social life?

Do you mean going out with your mates and having a tot and all that crap? All my friends I grew up with, from infants, they've all settled down, got two or three kids and that. Nice job, nice clothes, nice house, nice car, and they don't want to know me. They see me in the street and they cross the road, walk on the other side. 'Fuckin' hell, look at the fuckin' state of him. I don't want to be seen with him, he's a menace to society. Look at the dirt on his jeans, dirt on his shirt, and the glue bag he's got hanging out of his jacket.'

(Martin, aged 24)

Most respondents claimed that they did not care what people thought of them, that they had more urgent things to think about. At the same time, they did talk in a very reflective manner about their sense of themselves as homeless people, of the public response to them and the effect that their situation and the public response to it seemed to have on their self-esteem and their capacity for making and maintaining relationships with other people. The vast majority talked about their need for socializing in terms of a desperate need to pass the time. Without jobs or homes, the street homeless depended on the society of others to help them get through the day:

Different people do different things. Some people just sit in the day centres all day. Other people'll drink, other people'll take drugs.

Some people look for work, but you give that up after a couple of months.

(Jack, aged 23)

You look forward to Friday. Cos you're unemployed you've got that much time on your hands – a lot of people get up for their breakfast and go back to bed! Get up for their tea and just sit in front of the telly all night. Do the same the next day. It's just the time aspect. You've got so much time on your hands because you haven't got a job. You look forward to Friday, then on Friday you won't come back, get to sleep about three or four on a Saturday, sleep Saturday, sleep Sunday, then it's Monday. And you start again, waiting for Friday.

(Brian, aged 23)

All sociability is fraught with danger when you live on the streets. It's difficult to trust any person, it's difficult to trust any place, and even the activities you enjoy, and the people you do trust are more likely than not to be risky in terms of their violence-inducing or lawbreaking potential.

No, I don't trust no one, to be honest. You can't trust no one. When you've slept rough and had the same sorta life, you tend to trust no one again. They all just back off. When you're on your arse they don't wanna know.

(Neill, aged 21)

Don't trust no one. Because the way I see it, there's always someone there to stab you in the back. Bitter experience: trust no one, suspect everyone.

(Steve, aged 24)

Mike had a steady girlfriend on whom he was pinning many of his hopes for the future, but he dared not tell her he was in a hostel for the homeless:

I've not told her where I am, actually. It's a lie, and I hate lying. But rather than say, 'Look, I'm homeless', I told her I'm with a friend. You can understand that, can't you?

(Mike, aged 23)

Several of the young people knew they took risks on occasions when they were desperate to talk to someone – anyone.

How do I meet my friends? It's like when I'm begging, and asking people for a cigarette. People come up to me and talk to me for hours. They sit there for hours and don't shut up. So I have to put up with people talking to me for hours.

(Sue, aged 17)

It's always mixed feelings. Some people sit down and chat with you and treat you the same. Other people just look down on you as if you're rubbish and you're a waster and bad.

(Eddie, aged 23)

Others were more circumspect about the places they frequent, the types of relationship they negotiate:

I hang around by the actual centre, by the libraries and the museums. I never hang around where there's shops, because you're likely to get arrested there.

(Ralph, aged 23)

I stay clear of everyone, me. I talk to everyone, but there's certain people I like to steer clear of, like pimps, and what haveya and druggies. I think that if I start talking to a druggie, I'd get influenced by it, I'd wanna take it. I try to steer clear of them once I know they're a druggie.

(Ron, aged 17)

I know gay people that are ex-rent boys. I don't care what their lifestyle is. I've said, 'I don't care what your lifestyle is, so long as you don't touch me.'

(Wayne, aged 23)

Making sense of self and society

One of the objectives of the Three Cities Project was to assess what young homeless people think of themselves and the Society that they are both within and outwith. And, as we discovered from the descriptions of their experiences living rough, the space in which contemporary young homeless people can legitimately make sense of themselves, their lives, and the social relationships that help shape both, tends to get smaller and smaller as the general public learns to accommodate substantial numbers of them on the streets, and the regulatory agents of both commercial and enforcement agencies keep them under close surveillance. Because of their lack of residence and address the homeless young are pushed in on themselves in ever-decreasing circles of exclusion from civic and social life.

The individualistic philosophies of the Conservative government in 1980s Britain were dominant during the most formative years of today's young homeless people. It is not surprising, therefore, that when the interviewees were asked if they blamed anyone or anything for their present circumstances, 64 per cent (43) of the 67 who answered the question blamed themselves – with only 19 per cent (13) blaming the government/social services/'state', and 16 per cent (11) their families. Even so, the reasons for blaming themselves seemed to stem less from a conviction that they had ever done anything wrong enough to merit such harsh punishment, and more from a desperate and proud insistence that, given the unbearable circumstances in which they had found themselves, they had, in choosing to leave home, demonstrated a laudable independence, agency and a capacity to survive.

At the same time, none of the roofless people thought that they deserved to be suffering such an extreme degree of material deprivation. Yet the very feeling of being so outcast, and in part by choice, made it difficult for them to see how they could get back in – a not surprising sentiment, given the vulgar individualism vigorously promoted during the 1980s when Prime Minister Thatcher claimed that there is no such thing as Society! Regrettably, that latter *aperçu* became a self-fulfilling prophecy in respect of many of the victims of Thatcherite social policy. The anti-welfarist policies of Mrs Thatcher's governments (see previous chapter) ensured that many of the children of the 1980s who suffered the multiple disadvantages of unemployment, homelessness, poverty, and sexual and/or physical abuse, now have no viable sense of either themselves *or* Society. Yet . . . and yet, the young homeless have an overwhelming experience of being straitjacketed by innumerable bureaucratic rules and regulations as they try to get their welfare entitlements, of being subject to all kinds of regulatory officialdom as they move about the cities and the shires. They have, too, a weary cynicism about both those who make the rules and those who enforce them. Moreover, youth homelessness is now so extensive that the homeless are no longer only on the margins. The 'margins' have come to the centre, and their understanding of what is happening there (refracted via the mass media and consumer culture's self-perpetuating advertising portrayals of its winners and losers) has driven them still further in upon themselves. (Maybe this is why so many of the young people talked of society as if they feel that it is *imploding* – see below.) For, whereas from the late nineteenth century to the 1980s ideological control of the poor was increasingly of a modernist and disciplinary nature (with the emphasis on state controls and intervention), the deregulationist and crude market ideologies of the Thatcher years emphasized a postmodernist contra-disciplinarity – all rules are malleable; winner takes all, losers, 'tough it out'!

Unfortunately for the homeless (and strictly and literally speaking) contra-disciplinarity in the *social* relations of capitalist, bureaucratized societies (as opposed to contra-disciplinarity in art or science) is always and already anti-social. The very rules that are constantly under an erasure by the powerful, continue to operate systematically to the disadvantage of the always and already less powerful, and this asymmetry of rule usage is, of course, another indication of citizenship asymmetry.

Apparently, it was their sense of being in a 'no win' situation that led the young people to feel that they were both outwith and within politics: 'outwith' insofar as they had no faith in ever being able to better their own lives via the ballot box; 'within', because of an awareness of the gap between the moral rhetoric of social justice that had continued to be peddled even under the Thatcher governments (after all, Mrs Thatcher did liken herself to St Francis of Assisi when she came to power in 1979) and the actual political ideologies and policies that had deliberately targeted young unemployed school-leavers for pauperization. When Brian (aged 23) was asked whom he blamed for his situation, he replied:

> To me, personally, it's a mixture. In a way it's my fault, in a way it's the government's. My fault because I didn't get the qualifications to get a steady job, the government's fault for not giving companies support to keep them going – that put more people on the dole. They've changed a lot of the laws about the support that the unem-ployed get, and they brought out the law that 16–17-year-olds weren't to get dole money. And there's a lot of 16–17-year-olds in here have difficulty in getting their Housing Benefit.

We asked 85 of the young people the question: If you could vote in a general election tomorrow, would you go along and vote? (The wording allowed those who were below voting age to give a positive answer.) Sixty-four per cent of them (54) said that they wouldn't vote, the main reasons being either that they trusted no government, or that it made no differ-ence which party is nominally in power – none of them can make any difference. However, others just stated that voting was not something they did, and two made it quite explicit that they did not understand the ques-tion – one indicating that he thought that voting involved appearing on television, and the other, after 'voting' had been explained to her, saying that it sounded a good idea, but that she had never heard of it before. One person said that he would not feel competent to vote because while he was roofless he lacked opportunity to see either newspapers or television, and therefore had no information about the various party manifestos. Of the 31 who said they would vote, 20 claimed they would vote for Labour, 7 for the Green Party, 3 for the Liberal Democrats and 1 for the Conservatives. Overall, the dominant view, shared by both 'non-voters' and 'voters', was that policians are not to be trusted.

> I don't trust politicians, I don't deal with them. They say they're gonna do something, they lie. They're just corrupted. I don't care about the different parties, I don't trust none of them.
>
> (Clive, aged 18)

> I didn't vote; I don't trust them. I didn't bother to vote because you hear so many lies.
>
> (Alec, aged 26)

> I wouldn't vote, because I've found they're all as bad as each other. They make all these promises before they get in, they get in and they don't give a toss.
>
> (Steve, aged 24)

Not many people of our age are interested in politicians at all. Cos they're full of lies, they're very devious, aren't they? That's why not many people vote at our age.

(Bill, aged 19)

I just don't know how to vote, because they're saying they're going to do this and they never get it done anyway. It's just empty promises. So I'll probably stay out of it and won't vote.

(Kylie, aged 17)

The parties are all wankers. They haven't got a clue.

(Mac, aged 20)

However, a strong critique of the present Conservative government was proffered by a number of respondents:

I blame the government. They say they are doing something, but they just can't be bothered. They're too busy building nuclear stuff, trying to blow up the place before they look at the people who are living there.

(Kylie, aged 17)

Who do I blame? I blame the government. The government has got enough money and enough power to build places. Why the fuck don't they? I don't blame the people, I blame the government.

(Dora, aged 19)

I think it's Mr Major's fault myself. I mean there's enough fucking money being wasted on this and that. For fuck's sake! Everybody deserves some winnings. I mean the Tories have brought this country to its knees. I would vote, yeh. But certainly not for the Conservatives. 'Back to basics'! [Laughs] It's a joke, ain't it?

(Vince, aged 26)

I'd vote Labour. Because my personal view is that the country's gone to pot. There's millions unemployed (but they're massaging the figures) and my government are constantly telling lies.

(Kevin, aged 25)

If it weren't for the government we wouldn't be in this state now.

(Ralph, aged 23)

A class analysis was hinted at both by some of those who would not vote and by some of those who would:

Been like this all my life. I'm homeless, no matter what.

(Angie, aged 25)

I would vote Labour, because I think they try to do more for people who haven't got a lot or are homeless, like our class round here. Whereas the government seem to be more for the upper class.

(Dean, aged 21)

Labour caters more for our kinda people. Conservatives just look after their own.

(Bram, aged 24)

Conservative policies stink; ever since they've been in power like, making the rich richer and the poor poorer. They need to take a look at themselves.

(Wayne, aged 23)

The rich vote Tory because Labour wanted to tax them 50 per cent and they didn't like it. Labour is only saying 25 per cent for us – the unemployed – and 50 per cent for the rich people. But the rich people go: 'No, we're not having none of that. You can take their 50, but you're not having 50 per cent of mine.'

(Alan, aged 20)

[I would vote] Labour. Cos the Conservatives want to privatize the whole system, privatize the schools and education.

(Jock, aged 23)

I'd vote for the Green Party. The homeless problem's been growing long before the Conservatives got in. They haven't helped the issue! I mean, there was a massive rush for people to buy their own house and when there's a slump the government don't really help. A lot of people have found themselves homeless because they have failed at work, or they just haven't been able to meet the payments. Instead of assistance being offered to them people so that they could continue, they've just had snatchbacks. That's the capitalist state! That's the way it works, isn't it?

(Kirk, aged 25)

The government must know that they can't treat people like second class citizens, which they are doing. Those that want accommodation should have accommodation. It's your right as a British citizen. The country's rich enough. Government don't mean that you rule people; you're their servant. When you come to 10 Downing Street, you don't come to govern, you should come to be governed.

(Richard, aged 23)

I think about it but I still don't understand it. When you're walking up the road and you see all those empty houses, then you walk further down the road, and you see people sleeping on the street. You think, 'Why? Why?' They [government] can't tell people they ain't got no money, because look how much some people get for doing nothing! You see people getting a million for this and a million for that – for doing what? And there's people sleeping on the street. It's just not fair.

(Kylie, aged 17)

I remember I read something once about the Conservative MP who said, 'Oh, the homeless! That's the people you step over when you come out of the opera, isn't it?' You know, I thought, 'God! They're the people's that ruling us'.

And then ya get the aristocracy and the landowners, who're meant to be more civilized than people like me on the street – we're just shit. But they'll get on horses, they'll have a bit to drink, and they'll get a pack of dogs and chase a fox all over the country, and then they'll let the dogs rip it to shreds. And if they've got any young children there, they'll paint blood on their faces. But they're more civilized than us! [Laughs derisively] Think not.

(Judy, aged 21)

Judy and at least two other respondents were fundamentally at odds with the premises on which western societies are predicated:

A lot of stuff doesn't make much sense to me. I think they should pay attention to looking after the planet more, but all they seem to worry about is the economy. It doesn't matter if all your trees are dying and your lands are turning to desert . . . if you've got the economy, it's all right.

(Judy, aged 21)

I'd give all black people and Asian people the same rights as white people; all females the same rights as males. We'd tax the rich people more than we'd tax the poor people. I'd stop wasting so much money on armies and defence, and I'd stick it in the Health Service, Education and Housing –– which needs it.

(Alan, aged 20)

I don't believe in the way this world is run at the moment. All the government can think of doing is buying weapons. I mean, what's the point of going to war and 'fighting for freedom'? I mean, if they didn't build the bloody, goddamned things in the first place we wouldn't have war.

(Rory, aged 24)

Survivalism and exotica – when the margins meet at the centre

The survivalism of the young homeless in England is marked by ingenuity, stoicism and courage. Insofar as they strive to regain a world they have lost, homeless young people lead lives that are a mundane struggle for life's basic amenities, and sometimes that daily struggle takes them over the boundary of legitimate behaviour into the realms of crime. At the same time, their struggles are also permeated by a cynicism about the fundamental morality of a relatively rich society where some people are forced to beg, scavenge, and sleep in rubbish tips in order to keep alive. With no reason to hope that politicians will help them, the young homeless are led also to believe that the society around them is imploding and that they are therefore solely dependent upon their own resources. Cliff (aged 21), like many others interviewed, thought that increasing levels of homelessness must signal an extraordinary degree of social breakdown:

> It's gonna fold quite shortly. I know what the people out there are all about.

In the meantime, young people committed to survival continue to make their worlds more exotic. At rural fairs and festivals, in city squats, travellers' encampments, and on the streets of large conurbations and county towns, many young homeless people find a warmth denied them in more conventional circles. As part of survivalism, increasingly risky activities may include begging, busking, prostitution, drugtaking, drug dealing, more systematic and serious crime, and bouts of public drunkenness – with all the attendant violence and police intervention.

Summing up the connections between homelessness morality, crime and politics in a few sentences, Vince (aged 26) also resurrected the perennial questions about desert and citizenship, two concepts that are all too frequently missing from contemporary debates on crime. As they are questions that will recur in the next chapter, it is fitting that this one should close with Vince's piece:

> There's a lot of people going fucking cold tonight because some people can't be arsed to get up and do something about it. And I just think it's such a great waste and so selfish. Everybody deserves better than that, you know. There's a lot of people going to be stealing tonight, some people selling their bodies. That's fucking demoralizing. *Don't* they deserve something better?

4

SURVIVALISM, HOMELESSNESS, CRIME AND CITIZENSHIP

> The worst thing is that they don't see you as a person. They just
> see you as a homeless person – a thief, a robber. 'He's gonna
> *haunt* you.' They see you as a danger, a threat. Fuck knows why.
> Because you've got nothing and they've got something? That's
> probably it.
>
> (Colin, aged 23, 1994)

At the end of the twentieth century so many young people are excluded
from citizenship by the contradictions between the false promises of postmodern individualism (e.g. 'agency and reflexivity make winners of us
all'), and the anti-social repressions of modernist techno-bureaucracies
(which, when monetarist doctrines hold sway rationalize the pauperization of people surplus to 'market' requirements), that traditional explanations for the relationships between youth-crime and poverty become
at one and the same time both completely irrelevant *and* very relevant
indeed (cf. Lash 1994 on reflexivity). Crime theories that give primacy to
material deprivation as a 'cause' of youth-crime are rendered irrelevant
to policy-making by their nowadays redundant emphases on the normalcy of the traditional nuclear family and (later) the workplace, as prime
social institutions for the induction and enticement of young people into
responsible citizenship. (Forty per cent of marriages in Britain end in
divorce and the majority of young people leaving school cannot expect
to get full-time, long-term work.) Equally, the relevance of theories stressing 'cultural' (moral or educational) deprivation has been called into
question by a postmodernism that puts all cultural orthodoxies under a
continuous erasure, and by the new information technologies and mass
media whose surveillance and propaganda systems contradictorily
trumpet that 'knowledge is power' at the same time as effectively demon-
strating that knowledge is only power for those with the money to make
it work for them. There is still a class/caste system – based on knowledge-
production relations – and it is the persistence of this class system that
makes it imperative to take seriously the conventional criminological

wisdom about the relationships between crime and economic/cultural deprivation.

Implicit in all criminological theories of crime and economic/cultural deprivation is the question, 'How can anyone living in such poor material circumstances be expected to be law-abiding?' It might be assumed that the question is the classical one about the nature of reciprocal obligations between the state and its citizens. The various answers given, however, reveal that their sociological authors are more interested in the relationships between social structure and social action than in the state's right to punish, and all are variations on the following explanations: that poverty-stricken conditions lead to moral depravity (Bonger 1916/1967); that a disjunction between culturally legitimated aspirations and the structural opportunities for realizing them may engender an anomie sustaining self-justifying criminal activity (Merton 1957; Dahrendorf 1985); that under certain material conditions, lawbreaking behaviour is the normal behaviour for well-socialized children (Sutherland 1947); that middle-class trashing of the different cultural mores of lower-class youths provokes a male working-class celebration of lawbreaking behaviour as a way of resisting assaults on their self-esteem (Cohen 1955; Hall *et al.* 1978); and that because poverty-stricken people do not perceive themselves as having a stake in society, they have nothing to lose by breaking the law (Hirschi 1969; Kornhauser 1978; Carlen 1988). Actually, all the theories are much more sophisticated than that, and not one of them is as deterministic as they each appear in summary description. Nor do most forget to mention that it is sometimes more important to explain differential vulnerability to criminalization than it is to 'explain' differences in motivations to break the law. The only reason for resurrecting them here is because each presupposes a minimum of structural and moral certainty concerning the contractual nature of citizenship, but without specifying the political prerequisites for the differential degrees of citizenship conferred according to age, gender and race.

In the 1990s it has become fashionable to refer to the very poor and long-term homeless and unemployed as being on the margins of society, or alternatively, as constituting an underclass excluded from both labour force participation and the patterns of consumption available to the majority (Mann 1994: 79–80). Kirk Mann has cogently argued that the 'underclass' debate of the late twentieth century is but the old issue of the 'dangerous' poor dressed up in new clothes, that it is as much driven by fear of the poor as were the workhouse and charity movements of the nineteenth and early twentieth centuries. In presenting extracts from the stories of young, homeless people (interviewed at a moment in their homelessness in the early 1990s) within the context of histories of regulation of the poor and increasing punitiveness towards young people, I am trying to suggest that, though they are excluded from the labour and housing markets, the lives of today's homeless young have been shaped by: economic and political ideologies central to social policy since the early 1980s;

dominant modes of bureaucratic surveillance and changing conceptions of welfare and the obligations of the state to its young people; and punitive welfare and criminal justice systems whose routine procedures impact especially harshly on those who, through no fault of their own, lead lives that are particularly exposed to public rather than private (family or workplace) regulation.

Their stories suggest that they have the same aspirations to home and security as the majority, and, when in reflexive mode, the same range of personal values and moralities as are held by any other cross-section of society. They are as disillusioned about the morality of governments as are the rest of their age group; and maybe it is because they are so alienated from local politics that they express a greater interest in global issues about the environment and the control of weapons of mass destruction. Their struggles to survive, and the individualistic methods they adopt, are well in line with the 'anti-dependency' philosophies adopted by the Thatcher governments, the popular press and, more recently, sections of the Labour Party – as is the way that the majority of them primarily blame themselves for their predicament.

Their stories are important not because they are tales of exotica at the margins, but because they reveal how central government policies on welfare and housing have been especially punitive towards the children of the already poor – as well as to families already under strain. It is hoped that as a result of the foregoing analysis of the contradictions between prevailing ideologies of citizenship and the conditions of their realization, it will also be apparent why the homelessness narratives presented here are so frequently both possible and impossible, both plausible and implausible.

At the end of this chapter it will again be argued that the concept of asymmetrical citizenship is central to an understanding of the relationships between youth homelessness and crime – especially with reference to how an asymmetry of citizenship rights permeates and shapes juridical relations between the so-called underclass and the much-denied 'overclass', and also and concomitantly, between parents (and those whom the state legitimates as being *in loco parentis*) and their dependent children. Such asymmetries between underclass and overclass, and adult and young persons' citizen rights have traditionally, and most recently, been institutionalized by all the repressive legislation directed at the regulation of the poor, and at poor young males and single mothers in particular (see Chapter 2).

Furthermore, one most striking thing about the homelessness stories collected in the Three Cities Project is that again and again their young narrators had been victims of crimes and injustices at the hands of adults who would never be held to account for their depredations. Conversely, whenever these young citizens themselves had been accused of deviating from either the criminal law or social mores, they had received punishments of a magnitude out of all proportion to their wrongdoing. This conclusion has not been reached because the young interviewees themselves blamed anyone for their predicaments – indeed they mostly blamed themselves – but because, when aggregated, their stories present certain regularities of experience that give the lie to the following contemporary assumptions: that there is a homeless underclass with different values to the rest of society; that young people are a threat to society (rather than the other way round – see Brown 1995); and that youth crime needs to be understood in relation to *social* control. In denial of those discriminatory postulates about Britain's undervalued youth citizenry the arguments prompting the organization of the rest of this chapter are that:

1 Young homeless people do not constitute an underclass with moral values different to those held by any other cross-section of society – though their struggles to survive unpromising childhoods may have made them cynical about the extent to which those moral values have ever had (or will ever have) any political effects.
2 Young homeless people are a threat to society not because of their minor lawbreaking activities but because the economic, ideological and political conditions of their existence are indicative of the widening gap between the moral pretensions of liberal democratic societies and the shabby life-chances on offer to the children of the already poor.
3 The crimes of 'outcast youth' in general should be understood neither in relation to motivational factors, nor in relation to social control, but in relation to the 'anti-social' controls which, having deliberately excluded certain young people from citizen rights and citizen duties, in turn furnish the state with further justifications for abrogation of its own obligations to a youth citizenry denied.

Mundanity, exotica and survival crime

In Chapter 3 extracts were purposely selected from the stories of homeless young people to indicate that their fundamental concerns are the same as those of most people – getting a living and passing the time. The main difference between them and domiciled people is that they have to achieve these two fundamental human objectives outwith one of the major social props to self-esteem *and* state acknowledgement of citizenship claims – the address. Additionally, the present lives of many of the young people interviewed were still embedded in pasts in local authority residential care and abusing families. Thus reactions to very difficult childhoods had eventually and incrementally triggered survivalist lifestyles, from which, at the time of interview, the young people were finding it difficult to disentangle themselves, for three main reasons. First, certain activities, such as begging, prostitution and property crime, were still seen to offer either the only or the most financially rewarding way of getting a living. Second, despite their best efforts to avoid 'trouble', trouble was all around them in the form of police and public harassment, non-homeless, drugs and sex predators, and the sporadic violence imbricated in heavy drinking and drugs scenes. Third, they were loath to give up addictions that eased the pains of destitution by providing instant buzz, occupation, community and a consumerist lifestyle, when they could see nothing better on the horizon with which to replace them (cf. Collison 1996).

So ... on their own admission, 83 of the young persons interviewed in the Three Cities Project had been engaged in lawbreaking activities at some time prior to interview (cf. Farrington's 1989 finding in a longitudinal self-report survey of 400 London males that 96 per cent admitted to at least one classifiable offence by the age of 32). In the Three Cities Study, in addition to the 17 who did not admit to any crime (including begging) another 9 said that they had not broken the law since they had been homeless, and 7 more put forward begging as the only 'crime' they had committed since being homeless. Thus a third of them had either committed no crime or had only engaged in the exotic crime of begging ('exotic' because until the 1980s the Brits liked to think that begging is nowadays something that is only done in 'foreign' countries).

Another 25 young people were categorized as having committed only survival or lifestyle crimes. 'Survival' crimes – mainly minor ones such as soliciting and shoplifting, but some of them more serious, such as one-off and opportunistic burglary – are those which, their perpetrators argued, had been committed in response to destitution. 'Lifestyle' crimes – such as minor crimes of violence, possession of drugs, and vagrancy – are those which are part and parcel of the increased likelihood of criminalization to which people living in public or semi-public places are vulnerable.

The other 42 (including 23, that is, 55 per cent of those who had been in care) had been involved in a variety of criminal activities which could not be categorized as either 'survivalist' or 'lifestyle'. Fifteen had been thrown out of home *after* they had committed a crime, *after* they had been to prison or *after* they had upset their parents with unacceptable behaviour related to substance abuse. Altogether 24 of the 100 interviewed had become homeless *after* they had been involved in crime, but, as has been already stated, 9 of them had not been in criminal trouble since. A majority of the others had graduated from survivalist and lifestyle crime to more serious or persistent criminal careers when they had either immediately (or very rapidly) become homeless after running away from, or officially leaving, local authority residential care.

Thirty-nine of the young people had spent time in custodial institutions (37 serving sentences, and 2 on remand), and 26 (62 per cent) of the 42 who had been in local authority residential care had spent time in custody. Thus, of all those homeless young people interviewed who had ever been in custody, 67 per cent had previously been in care.

Overall, 58 respondents had had paid (legitimate) employment at some stage, 7 had been on Youth Training Schemes and 35 had never worked in a (legitimate) job. All the (legitimate) jobs had been low paid and unskilled and, in the majority of cases, part-time or casual (e.g. shop or market sales, construction or agricultural labouring, hotel and bar work, lorry driving, public sector low-paid service jobs). When referring to these jobs, the young people usually described them as 'crap', 'dead-end', or 'slave labour' – the latter frequently being the epithet given to Youth Training Schemes. Very few of those interviewed thought that they would ever achieve economic prosperity through paid employment in the future, and, given Barclay's (1995: 13–20) findings that the real wages of the lowest-paid young workers have been in decline since the 1980s, their pessimism was rooted in a realism authenticated by the most up-to-date research findings. Yet over half of them had tried to get work. Their experiences, however, had soon taught them that 'most low-income work provides neither upward mobility nor respectability to the very poor; it has minimal or in some cases no tangible benefits (Wagner 1993: 13).

All of those who had been homeless on the streets before the age at which they could claim benefits, together with those who had had difficulty in getting their entitlements or who could not live as they wanted to on the welfare payments made to them, had been tempted to engage, or actually had engaged, in begging or other types of survival crime.

Begging and the imploding society

Begging, more than any other activity of the homeless young, arouses a medley of mixed feelings in both the non-homeless and the homeless themselves. Its resurgence in Britain during the last quarter of the twentieth century has brought those who were slowly but inexorably pushed to the margins during the 1970s and 1980s right into the centre of public consciousness. There, as a visible sign of deteriorating social conditions, begging also causes anxiety and ambivalence about the legitimacy of the state's right to criminalize mendicancy. It is most likely for that reason that the 41 interviewees who said that they had engaged in begging at some time or another reported very mixed responses from the public, with all of them saying that they had received some money from passers-by, thereby indicating that begging is certainly not universally seen as a culpable or criminal activity. Diane, Rory, Lance, Dora, Kevin and Ian reported only good responses to their begging.

> The last time I was actually on the streets I done begging. I was trying to find some place to stay. This chap gave me £20. He said, 'Use that to find somewhere'. I thought that was really nice of him. This other chap bought me sausages (big sausages), eggs, a roll and a cake.
>
> (Diane, aged 17)

> The majority of people who walk past me give me some food or a little bit of money or some cigarettes.
>
> (Rory, aged 24)

I tell 'em straight that I am stuck for money. I says if you don't want to give me any that's understandable, but at least you could buy me a burger and a cup of tea, and you can sit and watch me eat it. People do give me money and I go and get food.

(Lance, aged 24)

I've asked some people for money and I've often made three or four quid. That'll get me through one day, get me some cigarettes and a good dinner. Like chips and gravy! Hell, that's a really great dinner! You think that's a fucking miracle when you get that.

(Dora, aged 19)

I done six hours of begging and got £14. They call it ham and eggin', beggin'! Some people feel sorry for ya cos you're homeless. They'd give you a pound, two pound . . . so I went and bought a meal at McDonalds.

(Kevin, aged 25)

I just raise enough money for a bag of chips. I usually get it. There's a chip shop up there, and they do chicken and chips for a pound. Now, chicken and chips, that'll do me. So, like, if I get a pound in the afternoon, I'll have chicken and chips and come on the night, about 11 or 12, I scrounge another pound and then do the same – chicken and chips – again.

(Ian, aged 24)

The experiences of others had been mixed:

When you're begging, hardly anyone, even if they're giving you money, will stop and talk to you. Then you get people that ignore you completely, or will be abusive to ya: 'Go and get a job', that's the usual one they'll come out with. Late at night, when they're drunk, they'll come up and kick you. Just get used to it.

(Jack, aged 23)

There is some kind people out there who do give. But others just start cussin' and taking the piss.

(Ralph, aged 23)

Sometimes I take all day to make £15 at the most. I walk round asking people. I once made about £17 and that was on Christmas Eve. Some people say they make up to £50 a day, that's a load of rubbish! You may get people telling you that at these interviews, but I wouldn't believe them. A lot of the public get a bit nervous when people hang around. Plus begging, of course, people get fed up with it. I did it for a bit, and then I gave up.

(Joe, aged 24)

Survival was given as the main reason for begging, though some respondents ruminated on the propriety of spending money from begging on drugs or drink, while others wondered whether they were justified in begging when there might be others worse off than them.

> Young people, because they can't get income support – 16 and 17-year-olds – if their mum and dad won't put them up, they have to beg, cos they can't get money no other way.
>
> (Jack, aged 23)

> I gotta go out there and beg – to survive. Well, I'd rather beg than go and break into somebody's house and make myself a breakfast. Yet you get arrested for begging. But the law, the society, the system is fucked up. (I'm sorry for saying this word, for swearing.)
>
> (Lance, aged 24)

Embarrassment, fear and pride were the reasons given for never (or no longer) begging.

> I have done it with my friend. I just haven't got any fun from it though, 'cause you get rejected. Very embarrassing! I think I made £1.20! [Laughs]
>
> (Vivien, aged 19)

> I used to beg. It was the only way. I didn't like it; there's no profit in it. And you're looked down on.
>
> (Alastair, aged 23)

> Shoplifting, yeh! But I haven't got the bottle to go begging. Fair play to them if they can do it, under the right circumstances.
>
> (Mac, aged 20)

> I'd rather starve than go out and beg for money . . . cause it's against my principles to go out begging off total strangers. My mum and dad still help me.
>
> (Mark, aged 18)

> I'd never do that. Never have, never will. I'd rather break into someone's house and steal food out of it. Impolite, begging.
>
> (Ron, aged 17)

> Robbed loadsa people for money, done loadsa stuff, done everything except houses, [but] I wouldn't beg. Just wouldn't. Never in me life!
>
> (Rachel, aged 16)

When begging, young people are at risk not only from random criminal attack, but also from police harassment and arrest:

It's against the law now, isn't it? John Major's made it against the law cos we don't have to pay tax on it. I've been nicked a few times, had me name taken.

(Arnie, aged 24)

They just tell you to move on, most of the time. But if you've done it before they'll take you in for it. Lock you up.

(Vivien, aged 19)

Yes, I've been locked up for it. Just got a caution. [Police say] it's against the law to beg, we ought to know that. But we just go on doing it. I tell them, 'It's either this or shoplifting'.

(Angie, aged 25)

I was begging and I got arrested. They tried to do me on begging, then they says, 'When was the last time you had a fix?' Do him on heroin, heroin addict! Then they went to search me for drugs, and they done me for being wanted at the time! So in the end they got from beggin' to heroin to being wanted!

(Richard, aged 23)

I've been arrested for begging. They took it to court and they almost got laughed out of court. Got a conditional discharge. You go in three times and they start fining you. And then they wonder how you pay the fine! You go a day without money, then you just come out of court and start begging again.

(Jack, aged 23)

I got fined for begging. I don't know how they expect you to pay it. I didn't. Couldn't afford it. Nothing's happened over it. There's not much point, is there? I don't know why they do it. It costs them more than £50 to arrest you, go through all the arrest procedure, and feedin' ya – if ya get nicked Friday, leave ya to Monday. Don't see the point. Think at the moment they gotta prove on paper that crime's going up, cos they wanna get the Criminal Justice Bill through.

(Carl, aged 23)

Been done for begging, yeh. Just a stupid law. It's an 1824 law: 'begging for alms' it's called. Really crazy! I got done for it four times.

(Drew, aged 24)

Drew's view was the dominant one. Interwoven into all their rumina-tions on the laws relating to begging was a key theme in their claims about survivalism in general – that insofar as they *are* victims (and in other dis-cursive contexts this was vehemently denied), they are in part victims of systems which, though their authority is rooted in claims to rationality, are experienced as being very irrational indeed.

Drugs: thrusting the margins to the centre

> *George* (aged 20): Well, basically with heroin, it keeps you warm. But it ain't just that, though, it's a nice buzz, comfortable. It's a good pain-killer. It kills the pain in your body, but it also kills the emotional pain in your head as well. A lot of people don't realize that.
> *Interviewer*: So it will get you through the cold nights?
> *George*: And through your boring days.

> People just use drugs because nobody wants to know ya, and it hurts. It's a screen to hide behind. I've not got a habit, but many times I've snuff off, and I'm not ashamed to say it. Like, if you call me names, it hurts me. But if I go out there and get something, I haven't got no feeling any more, I've killed it. It's not like, 'Oh, let's go out for a drink'. For me it ain't anyway. For me it's just a screen.
>
> (Barry, aged 25)

> It's a nice feeling . . . very confident, a confidence boost. One of the nicest feelings you can get, really – apart from having god in your life, I suppose.
>
> (Sam, aged 25)

Seventy-six of the young people interviewed said that they either used some kind of illegal drug or abused a legal substance such as solvents. Fifty of them used softer drugs only and 26 used hard drugs alone or alongside other illicit substances. Five talked of severe problems relating to alcohol only, and another 11 mentioned alcohol problems (mainly minor) combined with other drug usage. (Their frequent arrests on drunk and disorderly charges may have been more a reflection of the public nature of their drinking, than indicative of its intensity relative to that of people who do their drinking at home.) What they all stressed was what Mike Collison (1995) has referred to as the 'embeddedness of drugs' – that drugs are easily available to young teenagers and older people whether they are homeless or not (cf. Parker *et al.* 1995). This being so, they argued, their illicit drug usage is not peculiar to their homeless state, even though drugs might indeed be used to ease homelessness-related anxieties and pain.

None the less, the numbers admitting to using some kind of illegal drug were much higher than among respondents aged between 16 and 29 who completed the booklet on drug usage and knowledge of drugs in the 1992 British Crime Survey (BCS). In the survey only 28 per cent of young adults between the ages 16 and 29 said that they had ever used at least one of a list of illegal drugs (Mott and Mirrlees-Black 1995) compared with 76 per cent in the Three Cities Project. Certainly a high proportion of the young people interviewed in the Three Cities Project were likely to have had higher than average exposure to illegal drug sources at times when they were living on the streets or in penal institutions, though only the women who were currently engaged in prostitution complained that they were pestered by dealers trying to sell the relatively expensive crack cocaine.

> I think that anyone who wants drugs can get drugs. But maybe homeless people do try drugs, cause, fuck me! they got to get through somehow. We're not given the chance to think about work or trying to get a job or going to college – so on a day to day level they're just thinking of how to get through the day . . . so maybe they're more liable to try drugs
>
> (Vince, aged 26)

As Vince implied, in addition to being pleasurable, drug consumption provides (for some, at least) a rationale for getting up in the morning, an occupational framework to the day, and a sense of community and identification with other drug users (cf. Rosenbaum 1983). Drugs have to be bought, the money to buy them has to be obtained, and users can swap (often quite sophisticated) knowledge about the sources and effects of different substances. Only a few said they thought their drug usage was out of control. The majority of illicit substance users either felt that they used drugs in a controlled and/or variable way, or that they would be able to vary their usage when they wanted to. The overriding consideration was that drugs were readily available when all else had failed:

> If you get convicted of a crime you go to gaol, then you haven't got to worry about any of your problems. The drug life is still there, but your accommodation problem's gone. The drugs help you forget about that, and then the major problem in your life is where to get the drugs, because the drugs are easier to get than the accommodation. That becomes your main priority – even in some cases before food and personal hygiene. If they haven't got the money, they've got to get the money to get that drug. And if they're not in receipt of benefit, the easiest way of getting the money is to commit crime. So it's just like a vicious circle once you get into it. I know lads who come out of gaol and they're reoffending the same day just to pay for their habit. All they've thought about the whole time in custody is the next fix when they get out. Or they've continued with their drug habit while they've been in custody.
>
> (Kirk, aged 25)

The main complaint about drugs was that although they were everywhere, and undeniably therapeutic in the short term, in the longer term they got you nowhere and were irrelevant to what most of the young people aspired to – a life of their own – that is, a life over which they had control.

They make your life seem easier when it's not, and they make you forget what the important things in life are. All your priorities go out of the window. It comes back to not seeing the light at the end of the tunnel.

(Kirk, aged 25)

Survivalism and crime

I've not slept on the street; I've gone and broken into an empty house or something. I didn't have no money, no address to claim from, so I had to rob.

(Ray, aged 20)

George (aged 20): I've got to clothe myself, feed myself, and support my habit.
Interviewer: So what do you do when you run out of money?
George: Go back to thieving, to be blunt.

You can't survive on the money, to be honest. I can make about three grand off [stealing] two cars a day; I'd rather live off that than £60 a fortnight.

(Tony, aged 19)

When I get hungry, I do shoplifting. I can't live without food.

(Liam, aged 17)

They've got nothing, so it's natural they go to a shop, rob it and sell it to get money . . . I had to break into a few houses. One of them I just couldn't get into. So I was actually out that night, and it killed me.

(Peter, aged 16)

When you ain't had any food in your belly for days, the first thing that you do when you get your giro, you go to the nearest cafe and you get the biggest breakfast you've seen in your life – you know, five pieces of bacon, five eggs! [So], it's a very big temptation, really. If I've had no food in my belly, ya know . . . I might go into the market and pick something off the stalls and flog it to another market trader for a few quid.

(Martin, aged 23)

Burglaries, assaults, wounding, robberies . . . just everything I was getting locked up for. Just desperation, weren't it?

(Colin, aged 23)

I got a fine for shoplifting, because I was getting toiletries, cos I'd got no money and I didn't want to be smelly and feel horrible all the time.

You've got to go out and steal so you can buy yourself decent clothes, food, toiletries – all the things you'd have at home.

(Ken, aged 19)

I used to offend just to get into the police cells. Used to wait for a cop to come, just put a window through or something.

(Simon, aged 19)

It depends with me. If I'm desperate, I'll see a car, and even if it's alarmed – there's two ways I can deal with an alarm. But, usually, I just break the window and if there's anything on the back seat or the front seat, I'll grab [it]. If there's a stereo, I'll just pop the window, get the cassette. I get about 35, 40 quid. But, I really, really do need to go out robbing, to earn some money.

(Ian, aged 24)

Being hungry, no food, nothing to drink, no money and just stranded on the streets . . . When you start to get hungry, you want to commit crime, don't you?

(Kevin, aged 25)

You get these stuck-up bastards with jobs, who drive BMWs, vote Conservative and all that crap, who think their life's great. But if it was took away, they'd do exactly what the homeless are doing now, surviving. Any way they could, they'd do it. I did everything I could to survive. (But I never jumped no old ladies, man.)

(Keith, aged 24)

Seven (30 per cent) of the women and three (4 per cent) of the men said that they had engaged in prostitution in order to get a living:

I've done prostitution, yeh. You just stand on the street corners, you know, just waiting for the cars to come round, and wait for punters. And when they stop, just go over to them and ask 'em if they're looking for business. If they say yeh, you just get in the car. If they want a hand job or a blow job, it's £20. If they want more, then it gets more.

(Spanner, aged 19)

We used to pretend we were rent boys, but just used to mug them, take 'em in the bog and then rip them off. We stopped doing it because one of our mates got in a car, drove off in a BMW, and he had to do it. The guy was gonna shoot him if he didn't.

(Tim, aged 20)

I've seen a lot of lads come from going on the street to going over to be rent boys. Cos they've got no money, they've got no decent clothes, no food, empty stomachs, and they can't have a good time. That's the worst part of being homeless – no social life.

(George, aged 23)

For 15 minutes work, lie on your back, spread your legs . . . 90 quid. Makes you think, dunnit? Cos that's rent for a week in a flat, and then if you had a couple of guys like that you can get your flat furnished, your food. If you're good enough you could get a guy to buy you a flat, buy you a car, plus give you pocket money. You can do good business. Makes you think, don't it? If you want something in life, you've got to but look.

(Richard, aged 23)

You go into hotels and you blag 'em for money, cos some of them have never been in Manchester before. Like last night, I was with a punter and he said, 'How much is it inside?' I said, '£5, you're not doing it for less'. And I ended up getting £8 out of him. So I was all right.

(Rachel, aged 16)

Twenty-year-old Rosie said that she would much prefer to do prostitution than beg, adding by way of explanation, 'I just want to keep my dignity, that's all', while Dora, a year younger than Rosie, thought it was obvious why some homeless women work in the sex trade:

You've either got a home or you haven't. So you stand out there on the corner. I know 20 per cent of the girls out there haven't got homes. So it's obvious. The girls are out there for a home, to try and make something of themselves. Try and fucking sort themselves out.

(Dora, aged 19)

Lifestyle crime

Been dealing with 'em [drugs] since I was 14. Just depends on what the street's like. I was shoplifting just to feed myself. I wouldn't say I'm an alcoholic, but I like a drink. See, the people you know on the streets just turn to drink or drugs. It's not the life you really want, but you just stick with the gang. Got to get used to what they like, else they don't like you.

(Angie, aged 25)

Someone grassed me up for selling dope, which I thought was rather wrong. So me and my mate steamed round to his house, kicked the door in, and just beat the crap out of him with a baseball bat.

(Steve, aged 24)

I shared a room with a smackhead, and one night she just flipped her trolley, and she tried to stab me with one of her needles. I pushed her down the stairs and I got breached.

(Fiona, aged 18)

A friend of mine says to me, 'There's a couple of chimney pots in the back of this garden. You can get £10 apiece for them in a scrap yard.' So I'd gone round the back, expecting to find a couple of chimney pots, and I found a window open, and realized 'Oh, this is somebody's yard', you know, someone lives there. Before I could do anything – as soon as I walked round the yard – in those four minutes the police were on the scene! I just ran, and then they caught me about an hour later – up a tree! [Laughs] They said, 'We're charging you with attempted burglary!' I'm not into burglary, you know. I've never done anything like that in my life.

(Rory, aged 24)

Most of the lifestyle crime involved violence or substance abuse, but it was also often precipitated by an assault to which the young person would have been less likely to have been exposed had they not been homeless. Ralph was arrested after he and his friends had been involved in a serious fracas in a pub where they had been refused service. Several others had violently assaulted people who had threatened or criminally victimized them.

The person was homosexual and they tried, like, to get it on with me. I just didn't . . . I ain't fussed about homosexuals so long as they keep themselves to themselves. But if they try it on with me it starts freaking me out. I got a bit over the top and beat him up; and he took me to court for it.

(Ken, aged 19)

I'm banned for life from there [hostel]. I went in with a metal bar cos somebody took some money off me. Pinched money off me, so I went in with a metal bar to cave somebody's head in. They called the police, cos I was fighting with the staff. It's the principle. I don't like that done, especially when you're in the same boat as them.

(Ralph, aged 23)

Ralph had previously taken the law into his own hands in a dispute with an employer about wages, remarking ruefully, as he concluded the tale,

I didn't go to no Citizens' Advice Bureau. I should have done, man. But I smashed his face in.

But would Ralph's wrongs have been redressed if he had sought official help? According to their own accounts, a majority of the young homeless people interviewed had themselves been victims of serious crimes (cf. Brown 1995; Hartless *et al.* 1995; Maung 1995). These had seldom been redressed – even when brought to the attention of the police in an appropriate and law-abiding manner (cf. Loader 1996).

Out there

As the young people told their stories about homelessness, the phrase 'out there' featured frequently, not only to denote life in the streets, but also to refer to a wider world where people outcast from what is assumed to be conventional life have to make out as best they can without home and a living wage. 'Out there' life was tough, but, even before they had become homeless, at least half the interviewees had experienced abuse or rejection by parents or adults entrusted with their care. Nine had been sexually abused, 19 had been physically abused, and 42 had spent time in local authority residential care.

For some the abuse had continued when they were in care. Alec had lived in a children's home the head of which had been prosecued in 1993 for indecent assaults on children in his care. Jane had been subjected to mental torture under Staffordshire's notorious 'pindown' regime for children in care who continually truanted or absconded – a regime which was described by the official inquiry into it as 'a narrow, punitive and harshly restrictive experience' (Levy and Kahan 1991: 167). Colin suffered severe beatings in his Catholic children's home:

> St Michael's was Christian, Catholic. They're dead strict, all brothers. You got battered in there. Used to leather you, just leather the shit out of you. You know those bamboo canes? They used to lash you with that, man. Sore from that, and then they put you in a cold bath. That was just for cursing, giving it the mouth. You'd be sore, you'd be blistered from it. Just ran away from there all the time. Ended up locked up.
>
> (Colin, aged 23)

Altogether 50 respondents had been crime victims on one or more occasions when they had been homeless. Thirty-one had been assaulted or threatened with violence; 24 had been victims of property crime; 6 (5 females, 1 male) had been raped; 1 had been set alight; 1 had been kidnapped; and 1 had been urinated on by passing youths. Thus 40 (48 per cent) of those who had committed crime themselves had also been victims of crime, while 10 (59 per cent) of those who claimed not to engage in crime reported some type of victimization. Beatings and stabbings in young offender institutions and prisons were mentioned by several respondents (Howard League 1995). Additionally, those who had spent any time on the streets frequently reported rough treatment at the hands of police or security guards as well as being prey to all sorts of predators.

> They [police] pulled me up once. Had me fuckin' suitcase. He said, 'What's in there?' I said, 'Mind your own business, cos I ain't doing

anything wrong'. And he said, 'We want to open it'. He checked me suitcase, got in the van and fucked off. Left me stuff all over the floor; never put it back! And they follow you. They've got a habit of when you're walking on the street – they follow you.

(Keith, aged 24)

I was sleeping rough and this bloke came up to me and says, 'Have you got the time?' He goes, 'Do you fancy a walk?' I went, 'No I'm all right here.' He goes, 'Can I play with your dick?' I went, 'No.' Then he goes, 'I'll pay you some money.' I went, 'No, just go away.' Eventually, he went . . . I was a bit scared about him.

(Tom, aged 20)

Well, I knew he was gay and I thought I could handle it. He got me behind, went to some waste land and he just did it. I was suffering from depression and I couldn't be bothered to fight him off, plus he had a hatchet on the floor and an SAS dagger in his pocket.

(Richard, aged 23)

When I was in London . . . a man come up to me and he said, 'Do you want to work for me?' I said, 'Doing what?' And he said, 'Being a rent boy.' Well, I turned him down. He was propositioning me to work for him because he thought I was homeless.

(Kevin, aged 25)

Whereas only 45 per cent (35) of the men had had at least one crime committed against them since they had been homeless, 65 per cent (15) of the women said that they had. The women, moreover, seemed to be more vulnerable to predatory harassment on the streets, and some of them mentioned violence, threats and various types of duress (suffered at the hands of drug dealers and pimps) which they had not mentioned when asked if they had ever been a victim of crime.

I was offered cocaine, smack, heroin. They all come up to you when you're homeless, and it doesn't matter how often you knock them back, they'll still come at you, night after night.

(Fiona, aged 18)

When I'm working I always have crack dealers coming up to me. 'Do you want some?' They just get the girls and get them addicted to crack.

(Rosie, aged 20)

I've been begging and folk have said, 'Oh, give you a fiver for a blow job.' And I've said, 'Do I look like a prostitute, mate?' You have got more hassle with folks trying to buy sex off you.

(Judy, aged 21)

Wouldn't like to go on the streets again. A bad experience. Pimps start getting you beat up because you won't work for them. I took a good few tankins off them – yeh, batterings for saying no, that I wouldn't work for them . . . It doesn't matter where I went, they always found me, kept on nagging and nagging – and the menaces! It's not safe at all. There's no way to protect yourself on the streets.

(Fiona, aged 18)

Both men and women said that when they had complained to the police about crimes committed against themselves, or when they had reported swindling shopkeepers or landlords, they had been told either that the matter was one for the civil courts, or that there was nothing the police could do because of lack of, or insufficient, evidence. The overwhelming message was that the homeless young receive very little police protection when they need it. Bill (aged 19) told how this had been explained to him when he had had his hostel room broken into:

Room doors are being kicked off and all the rest of it. The staff have said to me that the police are getting very tired of coming out [there]. But then again, that's what they're paid for, so I don't see why they should be bored with it, really. Who else do you phone when you have been a victim of crime?

Pathways: circling the margins and traversing the centre

It should by now be apparent that the routes into and out of youth home-lessness and crime are many and varied. Yet, however marginal to society's mainstream life and central institutions the young homeless may appear to be when they are seen on the streets or portrayed as problematic exotica in tear-jerking television documentaries, the mundane stories of the people interviewed in the Three Cities Project suggest that the con-stituents of their homelessness are also central to the economic, cultural and political life in contemporary Britain. Today's young homeless have been constituted within institutions (like the family and the regulatory welfare bureaucracies), economic and cultural trends (especially increased youth unemployment and drug usage), and political ideologies (of indi-vidualism and market morality) which are not marginal but *integral* to British society as the twenty-first century approaches. Yet, as they talked, the young homeless people showed a commitment to making their own lives and those of other people better. Twelve of them spontaneously men-tioned that they would like to 'go to college'; many of them referred to seeing television programmes suggesting that other people were worse off than themselves ('at least we're not at war, being bombed' was a frequent refrain); while a seller of *The Big Issue* was one of several similarly employed who enthused about the joys of doing a *worthwhile* job. All of them wanted a home.

Each of the five mini-stories pieced together on the following pages illustrates a typical pattern of young people's homelessness: crime, criminalization and crime victimization. Each also indicates how the lives of these so-called 'marginal' young people have been shaped and reshaped by asymmetries of citizenship which have punished them for both their own misfortunes and misdeeds and those of their families, at the same time as excluding them from even minimal rights to sustenance, shelter, personal security and the redress of wrongs committed against them.

Why *asymmetries of citizenship*? First, because each of the tales indicates that while children and young people are disproportionately punished for their misdeeds, their adult exploiters and criminal abusers usually get off scot-free. Second, and to put it bluntly, because even when the children of the wealthy *are* apprehended for delinquencies, they are not punished by homelessness, prostitution and mendicancy – institutions which have always operated as the ultimate anti-social controls to keep the 'dangerous classes' in their place.

The five stories pieced together below were chosen not only because they are illustrative of the most severe hardship suffered as a result of early exclusion from home, but also because they are indicative of a survivalism that is both morally committed and optimistic. Martin was taking steps to give up his addiction to glue; Jane hoped to do a course in child care; Roy was working at getting on better with his parents; Julie, homeless and pregnant, wanted to give her child a good life even though she felt that she would only be able to make a decent wage by continuing in prostitution; and Wayne, who wanted to help other young homeless people, was starting a community care course to help realize that desire.

Martin (aged 23): solvent abuse > crime > care > homelessness

I've had so many jobs that I've lost through solvents. I think that's what's made me homeless you know, cos when I was younger, I used to be really bad. It weren't only solvents, I was on drugs. I was always coming home high as a kite with Evostick. My [foster] parents just had enough and used to phone the police. That's how bad I was. My parents used to kick me out all the time. Well, I ended up on . . . er . . . I might as well tell you like . . . I ended up on the gay scene. You know, pay the rent and stuff. Been a rent boy. Things got worse from then, meeting all these dodgy fuckin' weirdos. And then I ended up lying place to place, not only with women but men – only for a roof over me head.

Me parents [had] put me in care. I'd been in this one children's home . . . yeh . . . secure unit, and even they couldn't handle me at the time, [so] they shipped me out to a different home, because I was that bad.

Things just got worser, and worser, and worser, and worser, and worser . . . Car thefts, burglaries, [pause] spikin', credit card spikin'. I've been to a few gaols, [and] I've been to three children's homes.

I'd rather go out there and work but I can't hold a job down. The amount of jobs I've done! Tool setting, powder coating, milling, drilling, catering, roofing, repointing . . . But like I said, I'm not so much heavy on the drugs now. I mean everyone likes to have a smoke now and again, but solvent abuse, it's crap. I just wanna get off it, but people don't realize how hard it is to come off.

I don't enjoy, you know, going with dirty old men like, er . . . fuckin'. It's just the fact that I needed the money. Well, you know . . . phew . . . you've put me in an embarrassing situation . . . Some of them punters, you get some of 'em really rough uns. They're driving around in the cars, they wind down the window and you think, 'I'm in, here', and all that's going through your head is pound note signs, know what I mean? That's going through your head [and] you don't care whether he's got fuckin' VD. The only thing you're worried about, especially if you're living on the streets, is that money going through your head . . . to survive on. You don't care whether he's got syphilis or anything like that, especially when you're desperate. And I've come across a few of these dodgy punters – 'Oh yeh, I'll give you about 30, 40 quid, come and suck me cock like.' Fair enough . . . I've done the job and then he's just tracked on me, just disappeared without paying. Too late, ain't it?

I've been in and out of gaols, and I always find that you can get more drugs in the jails than you can on the streets. You can get crack, cocaine, you can get the brown, Es, As. I used to get tubes of glue smuggled in for me.

Sometimes you just feel like climbing up to the biggest tower block in Birmingham city centre and jumping off. And then other times I feel really good, even though I'm on the streets. Like that psychiatrist said to me, 'There's only one person in this world who can get you off [solvents], and that's yourself'.

Interviewer: Whose fault is it you're homeless?
Martin: Mine. I was a wanker when I was younger.

Jane (aged 17): family conflict > care > homelessness > crime > homelessness

It started when I was in care really. I didn't get on with my stepdad. I was running away, doing stupid things, skiving school, and at the end of the third year I asked to go into voluntary care.

I got into loads of trouble there. In the end I got a care order for arson, and I did two and a half years in care. I kept running away all the time. When I left, I couldn't get any work cos of my previous record. I got a YTS in the end, and I only stuck it for about two weeks. I didn't get enough money to pay my rent, and my boyfriend was in a bail hostel at the time.

I'd been seeing this lad for about 13 months, and he went to prison. When he got out he had nowhere to live and he kept sneaking in [to Jane's hostel]. In the end I got kicked out. We were on the streets for nearly three and a half months. Just sleeping rough, living on Hanley bus station. We used to have to go up Woolworth's, in the skips, and get all the sandwiches and pies, used to get all the packages if they were out of date. You just had to wear your clothes, once they get dirty, nick another lot and chuck 'em. If you've got no food or money, you've got no choice, really. And I was going out robbing, cos I could-n't claim – well I could claim 'severe hardship', £3.60 a day. I've had trouble with giros because I'm only 17. They pay it, yes, but it's only every four weeks, and if they think I'm messing about – not finding a room – they just cancel everything and start again.

He couldn't find nowhere else cos he'd been in prison, so we went to social services. They were willing to give us singles in different places, but we wanted to stay together. There was this one place my social worker found me about three months later – they take people on probation. We went up there and the rent was something like 20 quid and we were only on the dole. He was claim-ing for me because I was only 16 then.

We were having £100 a fortnight between us, which wasn't much 'cause we had to get all the food. Then we had all these lads come round causing loads of hassle all over the place, kicked a door down and nicked a stereo and we got blamed for it. Got kicked out of there. Then we all got caught for burglar-ies. He went to prison and I got two years' probation.

I've got a social worker. He just can't find me anywhere. I can't go on the [housing waiting] list cos I'm only 17, and people won't take from social ser-vices cos all the kids are in trouble and they are all let loose to landlords, aren't they? It's dead hard to find girls flats. They've got loads of housing set up for people who leave bail hostels, but they're all male – houses for males to move into when they're finished here, but nothing for females.

I've got a job sorted out – there's this place that takes people from bail hostels. I've got an interview there on Monday. It's just a trainee place. I've had loads of YTSs. I didn't like the work – catering, machining, hairdressing. I'd like to do child care. I'm just holding on here, until I've got proper accommodation.

Roy (aged 23): truancy > burglary > secure unit > homelessness

Between the age of 14 and 16 I was rarely at school. I was hanging around arcades. We were all into rock music, going to concerts. Well, my parents wouldn't let me , so I ended up going to Birmingham and coming in at three the next morning. Twice I got in, and then they locked the door. That hurt me. It was an absolutely frosty night, and I slept in the garden. I woke up and I was sick and cold. I walked out. You can't put your parents through that, but you don't realize it at the time. They wanted me to be at college, I just wanted to get out into the big world. But time goes by and you get left behind.

My father used to say to me, 'The first sign of police coming to this door, you're out.' He was fairly strict. [Soon after Roy had left home at the age of 16, he was involved in a burglary, his first and only offence.] I was in Longton police station after the burglary, and a copper came round and I said, 'When am I going home?' He said, 'Well, we've contacted your parents and they don't want you.' I went to a secure unit. After about three months I went to a rehabili-tation hostel. I stayed there for about 10 months and then went to bed and breakfast. Stayed there about three years, and then came to [this hostel]. I've had small things pinched off me here.

I've come to the stage now where I just want to get my own place. It's took me six years to realize it . . . If I wanted to, I could say, 'Bugger this' and do a bit of thieving – the opportunities are all there. I'm not going to, but in this country, you're tempted by everything – a gold bracelet, a video, a nice stereo . . . or someone going past you in a bigger car. I don't blame my parents; I see them regularly now and I could go back home. But I say, 'No'. I'm home-less because of myself, so I say, 'No'.

Julie (aged 24): sexual abuse > care > physical abuse > prostitution > prison > homelessness > drugs > prostitution

My mum and dad put me in a home and then my dad started abusing me. I only used to visit them at weekends [and] when my dad started doing what he did, I stopped going. From that day till now my mum doesn't know what he's done. No one would have believed me. The job is – witnesses.

At the age of 17 I met this guy in a children's home, got a house together, had three kids, he got on smack. Things went down from there on. I ended up going out on the beat, because I was feeding his habit. And I just got sick of it. I thought, 'Why the effing hell should I feed his habit? If he wants to take the drug he should go and do something for himself!' So I just turned round and said, 'Look I'm not doing it no more! I'm leaving you!' He got a gun to my head, and he sexually abused my kids in front of me! Now my son went to school and his back passage was bleeding and that's how they found out. Because I didn't go to the police straight away they took my kids off me, give me six months in prison and said I'm just as bad as him! How can I be just as bad as him? If they were put in the situation and they've got a gun to their head. . . ?

When I left him I thought, 'I'll be all right, I'll manage', but you don't realize. All I'm thinking of is where my next meal is coming from. Where am I going tonight. Now I know I'm pregnant, I'm going to tell them I want my own place. I wanted a kid anyway. But I'm frightened now because what have I got to offer it? Nothing! I'll still be out on the beat, because the money that the social will give us won't let us make ends meet. It's a circle.

I've been working on the streets now for 12 months but before that I was begging. Then I thought 'Sod this', and went into it [prostitution]. You're out there working to get the money to pay for your fines as well as food and stuff. We need clothes, toothpaste and stuff to keep yourself clean. Punters are not going to want to go near you if you smell. So it's just money, money, money all the time.

I wish I could stop it all! I don't like what I do, it makes me feel sick! I have actually been sick three times! I've got out from this car, really puked my guts up! There's AIDS and everything! So I'm dangering myself! I use Durex with everything, hand relief, oral and sex! But I've not done sex for nine months . . . other than with my fella! I just do hand relief and oral. The money's in the sex but sex is more risk! I'm not making so much money now because I don't want to do sex! When you get in a car with a strange person you don't know what he is! He could be a nut case, he could've just broken out of prison. For murder!

I've been approached loads of times out there. 'Come and work for me!' 'Come and work for me!' Believe me, I've been tempted because of scraping to find my next feed or scraping to find myself a place for the next day. I know for a fact if I go with a pimp I'd have a roof over my head, I'd have a square meal! But then there's bad advantages; he might try and get me on drugs, or he might try and get me into pornography and . . . You see what I mean? You think well, what if I go with him, I'm just going to get dragged down even further! Mind you, I'm a whizz addict as well.

Do you know that if a punter gets pulled up he doesn't even get charged? But he's just as bad as us. If we're homeless and they had legal places at least we would know that we were safe. But it does boil down to being homeless first, then drugs, then prostitution.

I've spoken to a lot of the girls out there and about six of us have sat in a cafe, we've all looked at each other and it's been, 'How did you end up getting into this?' And believe me, I can seriously say that not one of us can turn round and say, 'I love what I do!' We don't love what we do! It knocks us sick! I hate it! I feel dirty, really dirty when I've done it! But it's the money, and it's a good way of getting the money!

There's no punishment on this earth that'd stop me doing it! Unless they castrate me . . . and tie my hands back. Even if they start giving women imprisonment for prostitution it's not going to stop it because of the situation people are in today! Most of the people that are on the game are homeless! I don't think any normal person who was living in a house that had everything, would do it. That's how a lot of them end up on the drugs, by being home-less! And then into prostitution!

Wayne (aged 24): sexual abuse > runaway > drugs > crime > prison > homelessness

The situation that led to me being homeless when I was younger was because I was being sexually abused by my grandparents.

At the age of 2 I was brought over to England cos I was born in Belfast. Then my parents disowned me and give me over to my grandparents. From the age of about 11 to the age of about 16 I was sexually abused by my grandfather . . . I thought this is normal for everybody. It took me six years, up until the age of 22 to turn round and say to somebody, 'Look, this is the situation, I need help'. My head was totally wrecked because I'd kept it in my mind for six years.

At the age of 17, when I moved out and I started seeing programmes on sexual abuse and physical abuse and things like that, I thought, 'Well . . . that's happened to me'. But I didn't know anybody I could talk to. I couldn't tell my friends on the streets that I'd been sexually abused cos they'd probably just say, 'Oh well, that's it, you can't do anything about it now'. And I mean yeh, I can't do anything about it cos my grandad's dead. My grandad died before I moved out. But like . . . I moved out for another reason . . . cos me and my nan were having arguments. So I thought well, I'm going, I'm not staying here, and I went to live on the streets. I was stealing things from C & A and Rackhams, you know, stealing underwear, going to public baths and having a shower there, putting fresh underwear on, leaving the underwear there and just walkin' out.

I slept rough on the streets. I slept in mates' flats for days on end, em . . . slept on the back of Midland Red buses, on the back of coaches. Then, when I was 20, one of the older guys that I used to drink with suggested that I go to the Salvation Army and they'd refer me to somewhere for permanent accommodation. Stayed in there for one night, had all my meals provided, and then the next morning they says, 'Right, we can phone up for you, and provide accommodation if they've got a space for you'. So I went there for an interview and they says, 'Yeh, come back', like. 'Go to the DHSS, make a claim. Go to the dole office and make a claim there as well, and then come back here with . . .' with a receipt saying that I had been. 'Come back here and you'll have a place.' I stayed in there for six months, [then] they got me my own flat. I thought I'd got everything sorted but when I'd been in there for two years I started to get problems with my bills and trying to pay them, and I couldn't. I couldn't afford food. So my health was going down the hill, plus I was having trouble from people that lived in the area that I was living in.

Then I moved. I'd seen one of my friends and he says, 'You can always stay with me'. I've stayed with him for three or four months now. I feel a lot better cos I've got – I don't class them as friends, I class them as family. It's something I've never had properly is a proper, a proper family. Now OK, I treat them like brothers and sisters but they're my street brothers and sisters, they're not like proper family, but . . . I help with bills, I help with electric, I help with food, and I'm getting my head together. Plus I'm seeking counselling for my drug addiction, and I've been off it for five weeks. I don't need it any more, cos I'm not mixing with the people that I was mixing with before. Mixing with the totally different environment, where there's no speed, no ecstasy. Ok . . . yeh . . . I smoke the draw but I don't spend the majority of my giro on the draw. I pay bills, pay for food.

I've got a criminal record. I've been done for trespassing and burglary. There's seven warrants out for me at the moment, but for various things: two of 'em are for not paying fines, cos I refuse to pay fines. The others are for assaults. I hit somebody [and] I done three years inside for manslaughter. I was coming out of a pub, at the age of 17, and this guy stabbed me. So, I kicked him in the face . . . and his head hit the pavement and his skull just collapsed at the back. The police said I used excessive force . . . it's manslaughter.

My dad doesn't want to know me cos I've been in trouble with the police. My stepmum doesn't wanna know me, [and] my mum and my stepdad don't wanna know me either. I've said to them, 'You didn't care about me for the first 17 years of my life, so why should you care about me now?'

I'll be starting a community care course tomorrow. I want to work with people like me, well like I was a few years back. I'd prefer to work with younger homeless people because I feel I've got a lot to give them.

Interviewer: And what would you most like to own?
Wayne: What would I most like to own? A hostel. Yeh . . . for young people.

Preferably for couples, cos there's only one in Birmingham, and that's in Kings Heath. There's not any others anywhere else.

I'd never advise anyone to go on the streets, especially at this time of year, because of the cold, the snow. You're gonna get beaten up on the streets, you're gonna get abused in one form or another. You're gonna get into prostitution, end up being a rent boy, female prostitute or . . . a criminal.

End pieces: youth homelessness, crime, justice and citizenship

The only really notable innovation in underclass definitions has been the increasing flexibility of the term and its cancer-like tendency to expand in meaning, so that journalists and others add new people or groups who are thought to be acting in harmful or deviant ways. For example, when crack use became widespread, drug users were included in the underclass. The latter were often mentioned with the notation that they were often not poor – in which case one might add non-poor stock swindlers, embezzlers, and corrupt politicians to the underclass. In the past year I have also seen the term applied to public housing tenants *sui generis*, and to Russian immigrants being victimized by the lack of opportunities to learn English so they could continue their professional or other careers. It even came up in a feature about Mexican iguanas, which referred to those at the bottom of the iguana pecking order as underclass iguanas.

The behavioral definition of the underclass, which in essence proposes that some very poor people are somehow to be selected for separation from the rest of society and henceforth treated as especially undeserving, harbors many dangers – for their civil liberties and ours . . . for democracy and for the integration of society.

(Gans 1990)

In Chapter 1 it was emphasized that historically the two dominant motifs in discourses on homelessness have been citizen risk and less eligibility. No doubt many readers of the foregoing stories of young homeless people engaging in survivalist crime and drug usage will think that these youngsters obviously pose a risk, and that they should therefore be less eligible for social 'benefits' (labour market, housing or welfare) than those who already have them. (It is, after all, such circular thinking which produces the circle of deprivation to which so many of the interviewees referred.) Right-wing 'underclass' theorists certainly think that the undeserving poor should be excluded from respectable neighbourhoods. Murray's (1990) solution would be to ghettoize those whose poverty-stricken lifestyle renders them visibly different. Dahrendorf's (1985) liberal democratic plan, on the other hand, would be to 'define in' the young poor by providing them with real jobs and continuing education. The 'underclass' imagery used by both Murray and Dahrendorf is the ancient one relating poverty to disease and infection. Increases in the numbers of young women bearing and rearing children without men is a central focus of their arguments – as is a concern with the phenomenal growth in welfare spending.

At the level of feasibility, the proposals of both the right-wing conservative and the liberal democratic 'underclass' theorists are anachronistic. The right-wing conservatives recommend erasure of a postmodern situation by what amounts to the premodern solution of banishment. Behind liberal democrat recommendations for the management of poststructural ruptures and discontinuities in family and labour market are modernist assumptions about rational self-interest and the possibilities of shoving those already free of them back into old (and, arguably, now defunct) family and occupational structures.

As far as housing and homelessness is concerned, the continuing failure of British governments to recognize changing household structures is but a continuation of a process that began pre-Beveridge and has been aggravated ever since by the ideological refusals of all postwar governments to recognize the changing social relations between men and women, parents and children, and the changing structures of, and economic relationships between, labour and housing markets.

For Murray, the underclass menaces what he calls a 'free society'. For Dahrendorf the growth of an underclass poses a threat to democracy by reconstituting one of the historical conditions for totalitarianism. Yet it could be argued that the most menacing aspect of the underclass – and certainly the major threat posed by the young homeless begging on the streets – is that they fundamentally call into question the legitimacy of a rich, late twentieth-century, western democratic society which visibly fails to provide homes for thousands of its youth citizenry, and, less ostentatiously, fails to keep millions more out of poverty.

Any serious analysis of youth homelessness at the end of the twentieth century rapidly develops into an investigation of the irrelevancy and irrationality of the anti-social welfare surveillance and criminalization systems which in recent years have targeted unemployed and homeless youth for especial regulation and punishment. The most notable modes of anti-social targeting have been manifested in welfare cuts which were especially punitive towards young people not living at home with their parents, and in increased regulation (both at the techno-bureaucratic and the state levels) of all young people living outwith conventional household structures. The details of these anti-social controls on impoverished youth have been outlined and discussed in Chapters 2 and 3.

Yet the anti-social targeting of young people has diminished their citizen rights without enhancing the likelihood of pushing back their postmodern identities (rooted in experiences of risk, uncertainty and lonely individualism) into the idealized modernist moulds of familiness and wage labour. Closer examination of how the asymmetry of citizen rights and obligations shape unjust relations of juridical production between underclass and overclass (the latter's conditions of existence, incidentally, remaining predicated upon a high level of unemployment and hopes of a reflating housing market) suggests that in order to tackle the problem of the underclass, attention should focus totally upon the overclass that made them.

In relation to youth homelessness, crime, and citizenship the project should not be to 'define in' the young homeless by putting them back in their place in exploitative jobs and families, and thereby addressing them yet again as 'masterless men' in need of domiciliary and occupational control. Rather, the task should be to take seriously the contemporary asymmetries of citizenship which have helped spawn so many new, different and dissenting lifestyles and moralities then from poststructural diversity to piece together a new social ethics – a new ethics of citizenship for a new century.

APPENDIX

Ages and place of interview of the young people interviewed in the Three Cities Project

1 **Alec** is a 26-year-old man interviewed at a probation hostel in Stoke.
2 **Jane** is a 17-year-old woman interviewed at a probation hostel in Stoke.
3 **Brian** is a 23-year-old man interviewed at a hostel in Stoke.
4 **Mary** is a 17-year-old woman interviewed at a hostel in Stoke.
5 **Mike** is a 23-year-old man interviewed at a hostel in Stoke.
6 **Rita** is a 17-year-old woman interviewed at a hostel in Stoke.
7 **Zoe** is a 17-year-old woman interviewed at a hostel in Stoke.
8 **Roy** is a 23-year-old man interviewed at a hostel in Stoke.
9 **John** is a 17-year-old man interviewed at a hostel in Stoke.
10 **Geoff** is a 20-year-old man interviewed at a hostel in Stoke.
11 **Anne** is a 25-year-old woman interviewed at a hostel in Wolverhampton.
12 **Jatinda** is a 30-year-old woman interviewed at a hostel in Wolverhampton.
13 **Sharon** is a 23-year-old woman interviewed at a hostel in Birmingham.
14 **Clive** is an 18-year-old man interviewed at a hostel in Birmingham.
15 **Roger** is a 23-year-old man interviewed at a hostel in Birmingham.
16 **Alan** is a 20-year-old man interviewed at a hostel in Birmingham.
17 **Barney** is a 20-year-old man interviewed at a hostel in Birmingham.
18 **Ian** is a 24-year-old man interviewed at a Birmingham day centre for the homeless.
19 **Ken** is a 19-year-old man interviewed at a hostel in Birmingham.
20 **Len** is a 17-year-old man interviewed at a hostel in Birmingham.
21 **Matthew** is an 18-year-old man interviewed at a hostel in Birmingham.
22 **Sharne** is a 17-year-old woman interviewed at a hostel in Birmingham.
23 **Kylie** is a 17-year-old woman interviewed at a hostel in Birmingham.
24 **Wayne** is a 23-year-old man interviewed at a Birmingham day centre for the homeless.
25 **Colin** is a 23-year-old man interviewed at a Birmingham day centre for the homeless.
26 **Steve** is a 24-year-old man interviewed at a Birmingham day centre for the homeless.
27 **Rory** is a 24-year-old man interviewed at an advice centre in Birmingham.
28 **Mark** is an 18-year-old man interviewed at a hostel in Birmingham.
29 **Danny** is a 20-year-old man interviewed at a hostel in Birmingham.
30 **Tom** is a 20-year-old man interviewed at a Birmingham day centre for the homeless.

31 **Vince** is a 26-year-old man interviewed at a Birmingham day centre for the homeless.

32 **Jim** is a 22-year-old man interviewed at a hostel in Birmingham.

33 **Bill** is a 19-year-old man interviewed at a hostel in Birmingham.

34 **Diane** is a 17-year-old woman interviewed at a Birmingham day centre for the homeless.

35 **Fred** is a 25-year-old man interviewed at a soup kitchen in Birmingham.

36 **Judy** is a 21-year-old woman interviewed at a soup kitchen in Birmingham.

37 **Imre** is a 17-year-old man interviewed at an advice agency in Wolverhampton.

38 **Hussain** is a 17-year-old man interviewed at an advice agency in Wolverhampton.

39 **Joe** is a 24-year-old man interviewed at a Birmingham day centre for the homeless.

40 **Martin** is a 23-year-old man interviewed at a Birmingham day centre for the homeless.

41 **Jock** is a 23-year-old man interviewed at a Birmingham day centre for the homeless.

42 **Sue** is a 17-year-old woman interviewed at a Birmingham day centre for the homeless.

43 **Bob** is a 19-year-old man interviewed at a Birmingham day centre for the homeless.

44 **Tamsin** is a 17-year-old woman interviewed at a Birmingham day centre for the homeless.

45 **Ralph** is a 23-year-old man interviewed at a Birmingham day centre for the homeless.

46 **Eddie** is a 23-year-old man interviewed at a Birmingham day centre for the homeless.

47 **Laurie** is a 21-year-old man interviewed at a Birmingham day centre for the homeless.

48 **Spanner** is a 19-year-old man interviewed at an advice centre in Birmingham.

49 **Lance** is a 24-year-old man interviewed at a Birmingham day centre for the homeless.

50 **Mac** is a 20-year-old man interviewed at a Birmingham day centre for the homeless.

51 **Patrick** is a 17-year-old man interviewed at a Birmingham day centre for the homeless.

52 **Rosie** is a 20-year-old woman interviewed at a Birmingham day centre for the homeless.

53 **Kit** is a 23-year-old man interviewed at a Birmingham day centre for the homeless.

54 **Sarah** is a 20-year-old woman interviewed at a Birmingham day centre for the homeless.

55 **Richard** is a 23-year-old man interviewed at a Birmingham day centre for the homeless.

56 **Josh** is a 21-year-old man interviewed at Manchester day centre for the homeless.

57 **Kirk** is a 25-year-old man interviewed at a Manchester day centre for the homeless.

58 **Bram** is a 24-year-old man interviewed at a Manchester day centre for the homeless.

59 **Peter** is a 16-year-old man interviewed at a Manchester day centre for the homeless.
60 **Lewis** is a 22-year-old man interviewed at a Manchester day centre for the homeless.
61 **Julie** is a 24-year-old woman interviewed at a Manchester day centre for the homeless.
62 **Dirk** is a 17-year-old man interviewed at a Manchester day centre for the homeless.
63 **Alastair** is a 23-year-old man interviewed at a Manchester day centre for the homeless.
64 **Liam** is a 17-year-old man interviewed at a Manchester day centre for the homeless.
65 **Angie** is a 25-year-old woman interviewed at a Manchester day centre for the homeless.
66 **Dora** is a 19-year-old woman interviewed at a Manchester day centre for the homeless.
67 **Vivien** is a 19-year-old woman interviewed at a Manchester day centre for the homeless.
68 **Dominic** is a 19-year-old man interviewed at a probation hostel in Manchester.
69 **Mick** is a 21-year-old man interviewed at a custodial centre near Manchester.
70 **Frank** is a 20-year-old man interviewed at a custodial institution near Manchester.
71 **Barry** is a 25-year-old man interviewed at a street agency in Manchester.
72 **Melanie** is an 18-year-old woman interviewed at a probation hostel in Manchester.
73 **George** is a 20-year-old man interviewed at a street agency in Manchester.
74 **Leon** is a 25-year-old man interviewed at a street agency in Manchester.
75 **Jack** is a 23-year-old man interviewed at a street agency in Manchester.
76 **Arnie** is a 24-year-old man interviewed through a street agency in Manchester.
77 **Sam** is a 25-year-old man interviewed through a street agency in Manchester.
78 **Dean** is a 21-year-old man interviewed through a street agency in Manchester.
79 **Carl** is a 23-year-old man interviewed through a street agency in Manchester.
80 **Andy** is a 25-year-old man interviewed through a street agency in Manchester.
81 **Drew** is a 24-year-old man interviewed through a street agency in Manchester.
82 **Tony** is a 19-year-old man interviewed at a hostel in Manchester.
83 **Jake** is a 23-year-old man interviewed at a hostel in Manchester.
84 **Tim** is a 20-year-old man interviewed at a hostel in Manchester.
85 **Lynne** is a 20-year-old woman interviewed at a Manchester day centre for the homeless.
86 **Cliff** is a 21-year-old man interviewed at a Manchester day centre for the homeless.
87 **Ray** is a 20-year-old man interviewed at a Manchester day centre for the homeless.
88 **Charles** is a 20-year-old man interviewed at a Manchester day centre for the homeless.

89 **Rachel** is a 27-year-old woman interviewed at a Manchester day centre for the homeless.
90 **Vic** is a 16-year-old man interviewed at a Manchester day centre for the homeless.
91 **Kevin** is a 25-year-old man interviewed at a hostel in Manchester.
92 **Keith** is a 24-year-old man interviewed at a hostel in Manchester.
93 **Dave** is a 17-year-old man interviewed at a hostel in Manchester.
94 **Stewart** is a 20-year-old man interviewed at a hostel in Manchester.
95 **Fiona** is an 18-year-old woman interviewed at a hostel in Manchester.
96 **Ron** is a 17-year-old man interviewed at a hostel in Manchester.
97 **Simon** is a 19-year-old man interviewed at a hostel in Manchester.
98 **Rob** is a 19-year-old man interviewed at a hostel in Manchester.
99 **Neill** is a 22-year-old man interviewed at a hostel in Manchester.
100 **Ollie** is an 18-year-old man interviewed at a hostel in Manchester.

BIBLIOGRAPHY

Abrahams, C. and Mungall, R. (1992) *Runaways: Exploding the Myths*. London: National Children's Home.

Adams, T. (1990) *Bureaucrats and Beggars*. London: Oxford University Press.

Allard, A., Brown, G. and Smith, R. (1994) *The Way It Is . . . Young People Speak Out*. London: Children's Society/Beacon Press.

Anderson, I., Kemp, P. and Quilgars, D. (1993) *Single Homeless People*. London: Department of the Environment.

Archbishops' Commission on Rural Areas (1990) *Faith in the Countryside*. London: Churchman Publishing.

Arden, A. (1982) *The Homeless Persons Act*. London: Legal Action Group.

Audit Commission (1986) *Managing the Crisis in Council Housing*. London: HMSO.

Aungles, A. (1994) *The Prison and the Home*. Sydney: Institute of Criminology.

Austerberry, H. and Watson, H. (1983) *Women on the Margins: A Study of Single Women's Housing Problems*. London: Routledge and Kegan Paul.

Bailey, R. (1973) *The Squatters*. Harmondsworth: Penguin.

Banks, M. (1992) Youth employment and training, in C. Coleman and C. Warren-Adamson (eds) *Youth Policy*. London: Routledge.

Barclay, P. (1995) *Joseph Rowntree Inquiry into Income and Wealth*, Volume 1. York: Joseph Rowntree Foundation.

Barnard, D. and Bing, I. (1994) *Criminal Justice and Public Order Act, 1994*. Bexhill-on-Sea: Temple Lectures Ltd.

Barnardos (1989) *I Can't Go Back to Mum and Dad*. London: Barnardos.

Beck, U. (1992) *Risk Society: Towards a New Modernity*. London: Sage.

Bennett, A. (1994) *Writing Home*. London: Faber and Faber.

Bentley, I. (1981) Arcadia becomes Dunroamin, in P. Oliver, I. Davis and I. Bentley (eds) *Dunroamin: The Suburban Semi and Its Enemies*. London: Barrie and Jacobs.

Beveridge, W. (1942) *Social Insurance and Allied Services*, Cmnd 6404. London: HMSO.

Birmingham City Council (1992) *Strategy For Homelessness*. Birmingham City Council.

Bonger, W.A. (1916/1967) *Criminality and Economic Conditions*. (trans. H.P. Horton) New York: Agathon Press.

Brake, M. and Hale, C. (1992) *Public Order and Private Lives*. London: Routledge.

Bramley, G. (1990) *Bridging the Affordability Gap*. London: Association of District Councils and House Builders Federation.

Brown, P. (1991) Schooling and unemployment in the United Kingdom, in D. Ashton and G. Lowe (eds) *Making Their Way*. Milton Keynes: Open University Press.

Brown, S. (1995) Adult pasts and youthful presence: 'community safety', age and the politics of representation. Paper presented at the British Criminology Conference. Loughborough University, July.

Burke, K. (1964) *A Grammar of Motives*. Englewood Cliffs, NJ: Prentice-Hall.

Burke, K.(1969) *Rhetoric of Motives*. Berkeley, CA: University of California Press.

Burnett, J. (1978) *A Social History of Housing, 1815–1970*. Newton Abbot: David and Charles.

Button, E. (1990) *Rural Housing For Youth*. London: Centrepoint.

Campbell, B. (1993) *Goliath*. London: Methuen.

Carlen, P. (1983a) *Women's Imprisonment*. London: Routledge.

Carlen, P. (1983b) On rights and powers: some notes on penal politics, in D. Garland and P. Young (eds) *The Power to Punish*. London: Heinemann.

Carlen, P. (1987) Out of care, into custody, in P. Carlen and A. Worrall (eds) *Gender, Crime and Justice*. Milton Keynes: Open University Press.

Carlen, P. (1988) *Women, Crime and Poverty*. Milton Keynes: Open University Press.

Carlen, P. (1989) Crime, inequality and sentencing, in P. Carlen and D. Cook (eds) *Paying for Crime*. Milton Keynes: Open University Press: 8–28.

Carlen, P. (1990) *Alternatives to Women's Imprisonment*. Milton Keynes: Open University Press.

Carlen, P. (1992) Pindown, truancy and the interrogation of discipline. *Journal of Law and Society* 19(2): 251–70.

Carlen, P. (1995a) Virginia, criminology, and the anti-social control of women, in T. Blomberg and S. Cohen (eds) *Punishment and Social Control*. New York: Aldine de Gruyter.

Carlen, P. (1995b) *Young People, Lawbreaking, Criminalization, and Homelessness in Three Cities in Central England*, A Report to the Economic and Social Research Council, London: ESRC.

Carlen, P. (1996) Criminology Ltd: the search for a paradigm, in P. Walton and J. Young (eds) *The New Criminology Revisited*. London: Macmillan.

Carlen, P. and Christina, D. (1985) Christina: in her own time, in P. Carlen *et al.* *Criminal Women*. Cambridge: Polity.

Carlen, P., Christina, D., Hicks, J., O'Dwyer, J. and Tchaikowsky, C. (1985) *Criminal Women*. Cambridge: Polity.

Carlen, P., Gleeson, D. and Wardhaugh, J. (1992) *Truancy: The Politics of Compulsory Schooling*. Buckingham: Open University Press.

Carlen, P. and Wardhaugh, J. (1991) Locking up our daughters, in P. Carter, T. Jeffs and M. Smith (eds) *Social Work and Social Welfare, Yearbook 3*. Buckingham: Open University Press: 1–16.

Carlen, P. and Wardhaugh, J. (1992) *Shropshire Single Homelessness Survey*. Shrewsbury: Shropshire Probation/Keele University.

Casale, S. (1989) *Women Inside*. London: Civil Liberties Trust.

Central Office of Information (1993) *Housing*. London: HMSO.

Centrepoint (1990) *Carefree and Homeless*. London: Centrepoint.

Centrepoint (1994) *Statistics: Centrepoint*. London: Centrepoint.

Clark, D. (1991) *Rural Housing*. Cirencester: Action with Communities in Rural England.

Cohen, A.K. (1955) *Delinquent Boys*. New York: Macmillan.

Cohen, S. (1985) *Visions of Social Control*. Cambridge: Polity Press.
Cohen, S. (1995) *Denial and Acknowledgement: The Impact of Information About Human Rights Violations*. Jerusalem: Centre for Human Rights, Hebrew University.
Collison, M. (1995) *Police, Drugs and Community*. London: Free Association Books.
Collison, M. (1996) In search of the high life: drugs, crime, masculinities and consumption, in T. Jefferson and P. Carlen (eds) *British Journal of Criminology*, Special Issue, entitled *Masculinities, Social Relations and Crime*, 36(3) forthcoming.
Commision for Racial Equality (1992) *Annual Report*. London: CRE.
Cook, D. (1988) *Rich Law, Poor Law*. Milton Keynes: Open University Press.
Dahrendorf, R. (1985) *Law and Order*. London: Stevens.
Dahrendorf, R., Field, F., Hayman, C., Hutcheson, I., Hutton, W., Marquand, D., Sentence, A. and Wrigglesworth, I. (1995) *Report on Wealth Creation and Social Cohesion in a Free Society*. London: The Commission on Wealth and Social Creation.
Dandeker, C. (1990) *Surveillance, Power, Modernity*. Cambridge: Polity Press.
Daunton, M. (1983) *House and Home in the Victorian City*. London: Arnold.
Daunton, M. (1987) *A Property-Owning Democracy*. London: Faber and Faber.
Davis, J., Grant, R. and Locke, A. (1994) *Out of Site, Out of Mind*. London: The Children's Society.
Deakin, N., Jeffries, A., Meehan, E. and Twine, F. (1990) *New Perspectives on Citizenship*, New Waverley Papers, Social Policy Series No.3. Edinburgh: University of Edinburgh.
Dennis, N. (1993) *Rising Crime and the Dismembered Family*. London: Institute of Economic Affairs.
Dennis, N. and Erdos, G. (1992) *Families without Fatherhood*. London: IEA Health and Welfare Unit.
Department of the Environment (1977) *Housing Policy: A Consultative Document*. London: HMSO.
Department of the Environment (1981) *Single and Homeless*. London: HMSO.
Department of the Environment (1991) *Homelessness Code of Guidance for Local Authorities*. London: HMSO.
Department of the Environment (1993) *Local Authority Homelessness Acceptance Figures*. London: Department of the Environment.
Department of the Environment (1994) *Homelessness Code of Guidance for Local Authorities*. London: HMSO.
Department of Health (1989) *Children Act, 1989, Chapter 41*. London: HMSO.
Dibblin, J. (1991) *Wherever I Lay My Hat: Young Women and Homelessness*. London: Shelter.
Dobash, R. and Dobash, R. (1980) *Violence Against Wives*. London: Open Books.
Donzelot, J. (1979) *The Policing of Families*. London: Hutchinson.
Doyal, L. and Gough, I. (1991) *A Theory of Human Need*. London: Macmillan.
Drake, M., O'Brien, M. and Biebuyck, T. (1981) *Single and Homeless*. London: Department of Environment.
Engels, F. (1969, first published in Britain 1892) *The Condition of the Working Class in England*. London: Panther.
Ericson, R. (1994) The Royal Commission on criminal justice system surveillance, in M. McConville (ed.) *Criminal Justice in Crisis*. Oxford: Edward Elgar.
Esping-Anderson, G. (1990) *The Three Worlds of Welfare Capitalism*. Cambridge: Polity Press.

Farrington, D. (1989) Self reported and official offending from adolescence to delinquency, in M. Klein (ed.) *Cross-National Research in Crime and Delinquency*. Dordrecht: Kluwer: 399–423.

Feeley, M. and Simon, J. (1992) The new penology: notes on the emerging strategy of correction and its implications. *Criminology*, 30(4): 449–74.

Ferguson, D. and O'Mahoney, B. (1991) *Young, Black and Homeless in London*. London: Ujima Housing Association and Barnardos.

Fishman, L. (1990) *Women at the Wall*. New York: State University of New York Press.

Foucault, M. (1977) *Discipline and Punish*. London: Allen Lane.

Franklin, R. (1988) The demise of council housing: how should the probation service respond? Paper presented at Manchester Probation Study Day, 24 June.

Gans, H. (1990) Deconstructing the underclass, *Journal of the American Planning Association*, 56(3): 271–7.

Garland, D. (1985) *Punishment and Welfare: A History of Penal Strategies*. Aldershot: Gower.

Gauldie, E. (1974) *Cruel Habitations: A History of Working Class Housing, 1780–1918*. London: Allen and Unwin.

Giamo, B. and Grunberg, J. (1992) *Beyond Homelessness: Frames of Reference*. Iowa City, IA: University of Iowa Press.

Giddens, A. (1991) *Modernity and Self-Identity*. Cambridge: Polity Press.

Gilmour, I. (1992) *Dancing with Dogma*. London: Simon and Schuster.

Ginsburg, N. and Watson, S. (1992) Issues of race and gender, in J. Birchall (ed.) *Housing Policy in the 1990s*. London: Routledge: 140–62.

Gosling, J. (1988) *True Horror Stories*. London: Central London Social Security Advisers' Forum.

Gough, I. (1979) *The Political Economy of the Welfare State*. London: Macmillan

Graham, C. and Prosser, T. (eds) (1988) *Waiving the Rules*. Milton Keynes: Open University Press.

Green, G., Firth, I. and Chandler, R. (1988) *Women's Housing Handbook*. London: Resource Information Centre.

Greve, J. (1991) *Homelessness in Britain*. York: Rowntree Foundation.

Hall, S. (1983) The great moving right show, in S. Hall and M. Jacques (eds) *The Politics of Thatcherism*. London: Lawrence and Wishart.

Hall, S., Cricher, C., Jefferson, T., Clarke, J. and Roberts, B. (1978) *Policing the Crisis*. London: Macmillan.

Hartless, J., Ditton, J., Nair, G. and Phillips, S. (1995) More sinned against than sinning. *British Journal of Criminology*, 35(1) Winter: 114–33.

Hendessi, M. (1992) *4 in 10: Report on Young Women Who Become Homeless as a Result of Sexual Abuse*. London: CHAR.

Henriques, U. (1979) *Before the Welfare State*. London: Longman.

Hill, O. (1875) *Homes of the London Poor*. London: Frank Cass.

Hirschi, T. (1969) *Causes of Delinquency*. Berkeley, CA: University of California Press.

Hoath, D. (1983) *Homelessness*. London: Sweet and Maxwell.

Home Office (1995) *Statistical Bulletin, Issue 4/95*. London: Government Statistical Service.

Hope, T. (1995) Community crime prevention, in M. Tonry and D. Farrington (eds) *Preventing Crime: Criminal Justice*, Vol 19. Chicago, IL: University of Chicago Press.

House of Commons (1984) *Second Report of the Social Services Committee, Children in Care*, Vols I, II, III. London: HMSO.

Howard League (1995) *Banged Up, Beaten Up, Cutting Up: Commission of Inquiry into Violence in Penal Institutions for Teenagers under 18.* London: Howard League for Penal Reform.

Hutson, J. and Jenkins, R. (1987) Family relationships and the unemployment of young people in Swansea, in M. White (ed.) *The Social World of the Young Unemployed.* London: Policy Study Institute: 37–51.

Hutson, S. and Liddiard, M. (1994) *Youth Homelessness: The Construction of a Social Issue.* London: Macmillan.

Jahiel, R. (1987) The situation of homelessness, in R. Bingham, R. Green and B. White (eds) *The Homeless in Contemporary Society.* London: Sage: 99–118.

Jencks, C. (1994) *The Homeless.* Cambridge, MA: Harvard University Press.

Jutte, R. (1994) *Poverty and Deviance in Early Modern Europe.* Cambridge: Cambridge University Press.

Katz, M. (1989) *The Undeserving Poor: From the War on Poverty to the War on Welfare.* New York: Pantheon.

Killeen, D. (1992) Leaving home, in J. Coleman and C. Warren-Adamson (eds) *Youth Policy in the 1990s: The Way Forward.* London: Routledge.

Kleinman, M. (1988) When did it hurt most? Uneven decline in the availability of Council Housing in England. *Policy and Politics,* 16(4).

Kornhauser, A. (1978) *Social Sources of Delinquency.* Chicago, IL: University of Chicago Press.

Kosinski, J. (1992) Chance beings, in B. Giamo and J. Grunberg, *Beyond Homelessness.* Iowa City, IA: University of Iowa: 31–50.

Lambert, C., Jeffers, S., Burton, P. and Bramley, G. (1992) *Homelessness in Rural Areas.* Bristol: Rural Development Commission.

Lash, C. (1994) Reflexivity and its doubles, in U. Beck, A. Giddens and S. Lash (eds) *Reflexive Modernization.* Cambridge: Polity.

Lash, S. and Urry, J. (1994) *Economies of Signs and Space.* London: Sage.

Lee, D., Marsden, D., Rickman, P. and Duncombe, J. (1990) *Scheming for Youth.* Milton Keynes: Open University Press.

Levy, A. and Kahan, B. (1990) *The Pindown Experience and the Protection of Children: The Report of the Staffordshire Childcare Inquiry.* Stafford: Staffordshire County Council.

Lewis, R. and Talbot, A. (eds) (1987) *The People, the Church and the Land.* London: Ponsonby.

Liebow, E. (1993) *Tell them who I am.* New York: Macmillan Free Press.

Lister, R. (1990) *The Exclusive Society: Citizenship and the Poor.* London: Child Poverty Action Group.

Lifton, R. (1992) Victims and survivors, in B. Giamo and J. Grunberg (eds) *Beyond Homelessness: Frames of Reference.* Iowa City, IA: University of Iowa Press: 129–56.

Loader, I. (1996) *Youth, Policing and Democracy.* Basingstoke: Macmillan.

London County Council (1913) *Housing of the Working Classes 1855–1912.* London: LCC.

Lowe, R. and Shaw, W. (1993) *Travellers.* London: Fourth Estate.

Lowman, J., Menzies, R. and Palys, T. (1987) *Transcarceration: Essays in the Sociology of Social Control.* Aldershot: Gower.

McClusky, J. (1993) *Reassessing Priorities.* London: CHAR.

McClusky, J. (1994) *Acting in Isolation.* London: CHAR.

Maclennan, D., Gibb, K. and More, A. (1991) *Fairer Subsidies and Faster Growth – Housing, Government and the Economy*. York: Joseph Rowntree Foundation.

McRae, S. (1987) Social and political perspectives found among young unemployed men and women, in M.White (ed.) *The Social World of the Unemployed*. London: Policy Studies Institute: 61–86.

Malpass, P. (1990) *Reshaping Housing Policy*. London: Routledge.

Manchester City Council (1994) *The Report of Housing and Environmental Services: Housing and Environment Services Committee*. Manchester, 13 September.

Mann, K. (1994) Watching the defectives: observers of the underclass in the USA, Britain, and Australia. *Critical Social Policy*, 41: 79–108.

Manpower Services Commission (1978) *Young People and Work*. London: Manpower Services Commission.

Marcuse, P. (1988) Neutralizing homelessness. *Socialist Review*, 18: 69–96.

Marr, T.R. (1904) *Housing Conditions in Manchester and Salford*. Manchester: Sherratt and Hughes, at The University Press.

Maung, N. (1995) *Young People, Victimisation and the Police: British Crime Survey Findings on Experiences and Attitudes of 12 to 15 year olds*, Home Office Research Study 140, Home Office and Planning Unit Report. London: HMSO.

Merton, R.K. (1957) *Social Theory and Social Structure*. New York: Free Press.

Mestrovic, S. (1991) *The Coming Fin de Siècle: An Application of Durkheim's Sociology to Modernity and Postmodernity*. London: Routledge.

Meyer, P. (1977) *The Child and the State*. Cambridge: Cambridge University Press.

Millar, J. (1993) The continuing trend in rising poverty, in A. Sinfield (ed.) *Poverty, Inequality and Justice*. Edinburgh: University of Edinburgh, New Waverley Papers.

Monk, S. and Kleinman, M. (1990) Housing, in P. Brown and R. Sparks (eds) *Beyond Thatcherism*. Milton Keynes: Open University Press.

Morris, A., Giller, H., Swed, E. and Geach, H. (1980) *Locking Up Children*. London: Saxon House.

Mott, J. and Mirrlees-Black, C. (1993) *Self-Reported Drug Misuse in England and Wales: Findings from the 1992 British Crime Survey*. London: Research and Planning Unit.

Mungham, G. (1982) Workless youth as a moral panic, in T. Rees and P. Atkinson (eds) *Youth Unemployment and State Intervention*. London: Routledge and Kegan Paul.

Murray, C. (ed.) (1990) *The Emerging British Underclass*. London: Institute of Economic Affairs.

NACRO (1981) *Homeless Young Offenders*. London: NACRO.

National Assistance Board (1966) *Single Homeless Persons*. London: HMSO.

NCH Factfile (1991) *Children in Danger*. London: NCH.

NCH Factfile (1992) *Children in Danger*. London: NCH.

Newman, C. (1989) *Young Runaways*. London: Children's Society.

Oldman, J. (1991) *Homelessness: What's the Problem?* London: Shelter.

O'Mahoney, B. (1988) *A Capital Offence*. London: Routledge.

Onions, C. (1983) *Shorter Oxford English Dictionary*. London: Guild Publishing.

Parker, H., Measham, F. and Aldridge, J. (1995) *Drug Futures: Changing Patterns of Drug Use Amongst English Youth*. London: ISDD.

Pascall, G. (1986) *Social Policy: A Feminist Analysis*. London: Tavistock.

Pearson, G. (1975) *The Deviant Imagination*. London: Macmillan.

Pitman, D. and Gordon, C. (1958) *Revolving Door*. Illinois, IL: Free Press.
Pitts, J. (1992) Juvenile-justice policy, in J. Coleman and C. Warren-Adamson (eds) *Youth Policy in the 1990s*. London: Routledge.
Pizzey, E. (1974) *Scream Quietly or the Neighbours Will Hear*. Harmondsworth: Penguin.
Polyani, K. (1944) *The Great Transformation*. New York: Rinehart.
Pound, J. (1971) *Poverty and Vagrancy in Tudor England*. London: Longmans.
Prison Reform Trust (1991) *The Identikit Prisoner: Characteristics of the Prisoner Population*. London: PRS.
Randall, G. (1992) *Counted Out: An Investigation into the Extent of Single Homelessness Outside London*. London: Crisis and CHAR.
Ranson, S. (1984) Towards a tertiary tripartism: new codes of social control and the 17+, in P. Broadfoot (ed.) *Selection, Certification and Control*. London: Falmer.
Rees, G. (1993) *Hidden Truths*. London: Children's Society.
Robinson, G. (1990) *Conflict and Change in the Countryside*. London: Bellhaven Press.
Rose, L. (1988) *'Rogues and Vagabonds': Vagrant Underworld in Britain, 1815–1985*. London: Routledge.
Rose, N. (1989) *Governing the Soul*. London: Routledge.
Rosenbaum, M. (1983) *Women on Heroin*. New Brunswick, NJ: Rutgers University Press.
Rubinstein, D. (1974) *Victorian Homes*. Newton Abbot: David and Charles.
Shaw, C.R. (1929) *Delinquency Areas*. Chicago, IL: University of Chicago Press.
Shelter (1991) *Homelessness: What's the Problem?* London: Shelter.
Shelter (1994a) *Homelessness in England: The Facts*. London: Shelter.
Shelter (1994b) *About Shelter*. London: Shelter.
Shelter (1994c) *Shelter Annual Review, 1993/94*. London: Shelter.
Shucksmith, M. (1990) *Housebuilding in Britain's Countryside*. London: Routledge.
Simon, R.D. (1929) *How to Abolish the Slums*. London: Longman Green.
Simons, R. and Whitbeck, L. (1991) Running away during adolescence as a precursor to adult homelessness. *Social Services Review*, (65): 224–47.
Slack, P. (1990) *The English Poor Law, 1531–1782*. London: Macmillan.
Smith, J. and Gilford, S. (1991) *Homelessness Among Under-25s*. York: Joseph Rowntree Foundation.
Smith, S. (1989) *The Politics of 'Race' and Residence*. Cambridge: Polity Press.
Snow, D. and Anderson, L. (1993) *Down on Their Luck*. Berkeley, CA: University of California Press.
Stacey, J. (1990) *Brave New Families*. New York: Basic.
Stanley, C. (1995) Teenage kicks: urban narratives of dissent not deviance. *Crime, Law and Social Change*, 23(2): 91–119.
Stedman Jones, G. (1971) *Outcast London*. Oxford: Oxford University Press.
Stein, M. and Maynard, C. (1985) *I've Never Been So Lonely*. Bradford: NAYPIC.
Stein, M., Rees, G. and Frost, N. (1994) *Running – The Risk*. London: The Children's Society.
Stockley, D., Canter, D. and Bishop, D. (1991) *Young People on the Move*. Guildford: University of Surrey, Psychology Department.
Sutherland, E. (1947) *Principles of Criminology*. Philadelphia, PA: Lippincott.
Thomas, D. B. (ed.) (1932) *The Book of Vagabonds and Beggars with a Vocabulary of Their Language and a Preface by Martin Luther*. (first trans. into English by J.C.Hotten) London: Penguin Press.
Thornton, A. (1990) *The New Homeless*. London: SHAC.

Townsend, P. (1991) *The Poor Are Poorer: A Statistical Report on the Living Standards of Rich and Poor in the United Kingdom, 1979–1989*, Bristol: University of Bristol, Statistical Monitoring Unit, Department of Social Policy and Social Planning.

Townsend, P., Corrigan, P. and Kowarzi, U. (1987) *Poverty and Labour in London*. London: Low Pay Unit.

Twining, L. (1898) *Workhouses and Pauperism*. London: Methuen.

Von Hirsch, A. (1976) *Doing Justice*. New York: Hill and Wang.

Wagner, D. (1993) *Checkerboard Square*. Boulder, CO: Westview Press.

Walker, A. (1990) Blaming the victims, in C. Murray (ed.) *The Emerging British Underclass*. London: Institute of Economic Affairs.

Wallace, C. (1987) Between the Family and the State: Young People in Transition, in M. White (ed.) *The Social World of the Young Unemployed*. London: Policy Studies Institute: 1–30.

Watson, S. with Austerberry, H. (1986) *Housing and Homelessness: A Feminist Perspective*. London: Routledge and Kegan Paul.

Webb, S. and Webb, B.(1910) *English Poor Law Policy*. London: Longman Green.

Weber, M. (1947) *The Theory of Social and Economic Organization*. (ed. T. Parsons) London: Macmillan.

Wiles, P. (1988) Law, order and the state, in C. Graham and T. Prosser (eds) *Waiving the Rules*. Milton Keynes: Open University Press.

Williams, K. (1981) *From Pauperism to Poverty*. London: Routledge and Kegan Paul.

Wood, G. (1985) The politics of development policy labelling, in G. Wood (ed.) *Labelling in Development Policy*. London: Sage: 5–31.

Yapp, A. (1987) *First Come, First Served? A Study of Emergency Night Shelters*. London: Resource Information Centre.

Yeich, S. (1994) *The Politics of Ending Homelessness*. New York: University Press of America.

Young, M. and Halsey, A. (1995) *Family and Community Socialism*. London: Institute for Public Policy Research.

INDEX

ALTERNATIVES TO WOMEN'S IMPRISONMENT

Pat Carlen

Although many official and research reports have suggested that it is unnecessary for even 3 per cent of the prison population to be composed of women offenders, more women are being sent to prison each year. Moreover, although alternatives to women's imprisonment are continually (and ritualistically) invoked and prescribed, very little is known about the existing provision for women offenders and ex-prisoners, while even less is known about the successful projects and housing schemes which *do* offer alternative lifestyles to previously institutionalized and/or transient women and young girls.

Pat Carlen examines some of the fundamental issues concerning custodial and non-custodial penalties and overviews the current position of women in crime and custody. She reports on existing provision for women in England and Wales, innovative projects in other countries, and the impediments (both ideological and political) to reducing the female prison population. Finally, she outlines a strategy for the abolition of women's imprisonment.

Contents
Women's crimes and women's imprisonment: Current trends – Prisons: Preparing women for release – A home of her own: Accommodation for women in trouble and women ex-prisoners – Women together: Being, education, work – Women's imprisonment: Towards abolition – Appendix: Agencies, projects and hostels visited – References – Index.

152pp   0 335 09925 4 (Paperback)   0 335 09926 2 (Hardback)

WOMEN, CRIME AND POVERTY

Pat Carlen

I don't wanna go out there and thieve, right? But then I wouldn't have anything at all in my cupboard. So I say, 'Well, I'll have to suffer like everyone else,' – because everybody else *is* suffering. But sometimes it kind of gets on your nerves, suffering. Then I say, 'Oh blast it. I know how to do it. I'll go out there and get it.' (Kim, aged 28)

We used to sign-on on Thursdays and get his money on a Saturday. Sometimes it never used to come till Monday, so we was left starving. How can you tell your kids when they're starving that they have to wait till Monday? If I didna pinch it we'd have to go round scrounging. It were horrible. (Jean, aged 26)

All you learn in prison is kiting, smuggling and crotching. Basically, I thought about prison, 'What a waste of human life!' (Yvonne, aged 37)

I know more now than before I came into prison. I know about burglary, how to cut off burglar alarms, how to pick pockets. A girl here who's made a lot of money out of shoplifting showed me how to make a little thing out of a hairclip to take the buzzers off. And that Judge says it's done me good! (Kay, aged 21)

I've got used to it [Youth Custody Centre] so it's alright. I don't mind being locked in. I go to sleep . . . I dream. I always dream about the Children's Homes. (Daphne, aged 15)

Women have been pushed back twenty years since there came a Tory Government. (Zoe, aged 28)

Contents

208pp   0 335 15869 2 (Paperback)

PAYING FOR CRIME

Pat Carlen and Dee Cook (eds)

The fundamental purpose of this book is to examine the jurisprudential and sentencing dilemmas that arise when, in a society where income differentials are widening, the most usual penalty favoured by the criminal courts is a fine. When people cannot pay a monetary penalty they tend either to be pushed 'down tariff' towards a conditional discharge or 'up tariff' towards imprisonment. Sentencers are not happy with this situation: on the other hand they fear that when convicted persons are pushed 'down tariff' it appears that their poverty licenses crime; and, on the other, they are aware that imprisonment for fine default not only increases the already swollen prison population but also increases the likelihood of the person's reoffending. Yet, sentencers feel that 'something must be done' to mark society's disapprobation of crime.

Paying for Crime argues that, although 'something must be done', we must also re-examine contemporary sentencing myths that assume that it is only in relation to the poor that sentencing paradoxes arise; that see prison as the necessary and inevitable back-up to the fine; that assume the only viable alternatives to imprisonment are those transcarceral ones that bring the pains of imprisonment into the already-straitened circumstances of the poor outside prison. It examines closely the sentencing of women, of business fraudsters, and of tax and benefit fiddlers; throughout, it discusses achievable sentencing alternatives; and it concludes with a chapter which considers the alternatives to current penal policies towards offenders 'paying for crime'.

Contents
Introduction – Crime, inequality and sentencing – Monetary penalties and imprisonment: The realistic alternatives – Punishment, money and a sense of justice – Fines for women: Paradoxes and paradigms – Fraudulent justice? Sentencing the business criminal – Fiddling tax benefits: Inculpating the poor, exculpating the rich – Alternatives to and in prisons: A realistic approach – Bibliography – Author index – Subject index.

Contributors
Hilary Allen, Pat Carlen, Dee Cook, Michael Levi, Roger Matthews, Stephen Shaw, Peter Young.

176pp   0 335 09937 8 (Paperback)   0 335 09938 6 (Hardback)

GENDER, CRIME AND JUSTICE

Pat Carlen and Anne Worrall (eds)

Gender, Crime and Justice focuses on women's lawbreaking and criminalization, and analyses the relationships between the position of women in society and how women are represented and treated in courts and prisons. The arguments are explored in three main sections. Firstly, *Women in Crime* establishes the political and economic context conditioning women's experience of crime, justice and custody. Secondly, *Women in Courts* reports on rape cases, on how women are considered differentially when they request bail or commit violent crimes, and how women magistrates respond to women defendants. Finally, *Women in Custody* continues this empirical work, exploring how women are perceived and treated in care and in prison.

The contributors come from a variety of perspectives but together they examine and deconstruct the ideologies, discourses and practices that continue to ensure that women in crime, courts and custody are treated differently to men. Pat Carlen and Anne Worrall have brought together the leading writers in the field to present the current issues and research for students of sociology, criminology and women's studies and for professionals such as probation officers and social workers.

> This is clearly an important book and much needed in terms of evidence of injustice and discrimination. It is refreshing too, to find the victims themselves being given a voice . . . this is a good book, to be highly recommended to all those working and interested in the field.
>
> *(Community Care)*

> This collection pulls together some good, sound work on the subject of women and crime . . .
>
> *(The British Journal of Criminology)*

Contents
Introduction: Gender, crime and justice – Part I: Women in crime – Women and crime – Women on welfare – Prostitutes – Part II: Women in courts – Proving sexual assault – Rendering them harmless – The question of bail – Sisters in Law? Women defendants and women magistrates – Part III: Women in custody – Out of care, into custody – Women in prison – Women's imprisonment in England, Wales and Scotland – Bibliography – Author/subject index.

Conributors
Hilary Allen, Gerry Chambers, Dee Cook, Mary Eaton, Susan S.M. Edwards, Elaine Genders, Frances Heidensohn, Ann Millar, Josie O'Dwyer, Elaine Player, Judi Wilson.

224pp   0 335 15504 9 (Paperback)